Virgin, Mother, Queen

"This new Marian text manifests and celebrates a rich variety of Marian truth and devotion that will joyfully and efficaciously feed both the Catholic mind and heart. The artful combination of Michael O'Neill's professional precision regarding Marian apparitions coupled with Robert Fastiggi's encyclopedic knowledge of Mariology provides an inspired complement at the service of Our Lady and great spiritual wisdom to benefit readers."

Mark Miravalle
St. John Paul II Chair of Mariology
Franciscan University of Steubenville

"Searching for a book that contains everything you need to know about the most significant Marian apparitions in Church history? Look no further! Michael O'Neill and Dr. Robert Fastiggi have combined their knowledge of Our Lady into one delightful and easy-to-read book. In a unique and compelling way, *Virgin, Mother, Queen* presents the history, theology, and pious practices associated with the approved Marian apparitions of the Church. You will love this book! It is destined to be a reference work for years to come."

Fr. Donald Calloway, M.I.C.
Mariologist and author of *Champions of the Rosary*

"Combining their unique talents as a widely regarded Marian theologian and a 'miracle hunter,' Robert Fastiggi and Michael O'Neill, respectively, reveal themselves to be devoted sons of Mary in *Virgin, Mother, Queen*. This beautiful book combines history and theology both to deepen our devotion and to answer our questions about Mary's role throughout Church history."

Carrie Gress
Author of *The Marian Option*

"What a wonderfully gifted teaching and writing duo that have joined talents to help Catholics and other Christians understand more fully the role of the Blessed Mother. As a journalist who has had the honor of interviewing both of these powerful witnesses, I can say without a doubt that *Virgin, Mother, Queen* will be a true treasure that will serve as an important and creative tool for the New Evangelization."

Teresa Tomeo
Catholic author and syndicated radio talk show host

"*Virgin, Mother, Queen* will help many to fulfill the dying wish and command of the Lord Jesus: that his beloved disciples receive his mother Mary into their homes and their lives, so that she may help us in our journey towards him!"

Fr. James Phalan, C.S.C.
Former director of Family Rosary International

Virgin, Mother, Queen

Encountering Mary in Time and Tradition

Robert L. Fastiggi and Michael O'Neill

AVE MARIA PRESS AVE Notre Dame, Indiana

© 2019 by Robert L. Fastiggi and Michael O'Neill

All rights reserved. No part of this book may be used or reproduced in any manner whatsoever, except in the case of reprints in the context of reviews, without written permission from Ave Maria Press®, Inc., P.O. Box 428, Notre Dame, IN 46556, 1-800-282-1865.

Founded in 1865, Ave Maria Press is a ministry of the United States Province of Holy Cross.

www.avemariapress.com

Paperback: ISBN-13 978-1-59471-929-5

E-book: ISBN-13 978-1-59471-930-1

Cover image "LaVierge et le Lys" by William Adolphe Bouguereau. Photograph by Archivart/Alamy Stock Photo.

Cover and text design by Katherine Robinson.

Printed and bound in the United States of America.

Library of Congress Cataloging-in-Publication Data is available.

Contents

Introduction: Mary: Her Miracles and Messages
through Church History   ix

1. Mary as Blessed: Our Lady of Knock   1

2. Mary as Virgin: Our Lady of Guadalupe   17

3. Mary as Mother of God: Our Lady of Kibeho   35

4. Mary as Immaculate and All-Holy: Our Lady of
    Lourdes   49

5. Mary as Mother of Sorrows: Our Lady of
    La Salette   71

6. Mary as Mediatrix of Grace: Our Lady of the
    Miraculous Medal   85

7. Mary as Advocate: Our Lady of Pontmain   99

8. Mary as Mother of Mercy: Our Lady of
    Banneux   113

9. Mary as Mother of the Church: Our Lady
    of Fatima   127

10. Mary as Queen of Heaven: Our Lady of
     Beauraing   141

Conclusion: Mary in Most Recent Times: What
Is She Saying Today?   153

Notes   157

Mary: Her Miracles and Messages through Church History

by Michael O'Neill

Working on a map for a *National Geographic* cover story on the history of Marian apparitions ("Mary: The Most Powerful Woman in the World," December 2015), I was struck by the fact that the overwhelming majority of Vatican-approved apparitions have occurred in Europe. Only one single occurrence on American soil has ever been approved: the appearance of Our Lady of Good Help in Champion, Wisconsin.

I was there at the National Shrine of Our Lady of Good Help on December 8, 2010, with Relevant Radio as part of the live broadcast to cover Bishop David L. Ricken's historic approval of the apparitions reported on those grounds.

That unique and remarkable story begins in 1859, when a young Belgian immigrant named Adele Brise saw a woman dressed in dazzling white with a golden sash. (See image at left.) Twelve years later, on the same night as the Great Chicago Fire, another and even greater firestorm broke out in Wisconsin that destroyed 2,400 square miles and killed more than 1,500 people.

That 1871 fire was to become the deadliest fire in US history, driven by tornado-like winds. The fires were said to have licked the edges of the church property, but the church itself was among the grounds that were miraculously spared.[1] That night Mary, the Mother of Good Help, heard the pleas of her faith-filled children walking with a Marian statue in procession around the chapel, and a miracle happened.

As it turned out, this was only the first of many miracles to come. Inexplicable medical healings have been reported since the founding of the shrine. This renown for miracles has led to it being declared a national shrine and a true treasure for Catholics in America. One need only visit these sacred grounds to be reminded of the love that the faithful have for the Virgin Mary and their desire to learn more and grow closer to her and her Son.

The love and desire of Marian pilgrims form the subject of this book—how ten of the Vatican-recognized apparitions in the history of the Church point to different aspects of Mary and how these visions reinforce and emphasize the teachings of the Church concerning Mary and her spiritual maternity in the life of every Christian.

Each of the chapters of this book is dedicated to a different facet of Mary's ongoing maternity in the lives of all believers. In Knock, Ireland, in 1879, she revealed her blessedness as Our Lady of Silence. In sixteenth-century Mexico, the Virgin Mother appeared to the indigenous people (and, previously, in Spain to the Spanish) as Our Lady of Guadalupe. At different times and in different places, she has shown herself to her children in the way they most need her: as Mother of Sorrows, as Mediatrix of Grace, as Immaculate and All-Holy, as Mother of the Word, as Mother of Mercy, as Mother of the Church . . . and as Queen of Heaven. Each and every time, she calls us to conversion and penance in order to draw us ever closer to her Son.

And yet, these Marian apparitions are only part of the story. Because such phenomena fall in the realm of private revelation, it is possible in good faith to ignore these messages, which "do not belong . . . to the deposit of faith" (CCC, 67). Fortunately, we can rest safely with the Magisterium of the

Church, which presents the full revelation of God to us about Mary and her role in salvation history.

I was delighted when Dr. Robert Fastiggi agreed to partner with me in order to pair these two aspects of Marian belief: the private revelation of apparitions and the public revelation contained in the Church's Mariology. While I am known as the "Miracle Hunter," Robert represents the best in Marian devotion and scholarship, giving unparalleled insight into the scriptural and historical foundations for our understanding of Mary's unique role in salvation history.

For years, Robert and I have been members of the Mariological Society of America, a Catholic theological association dedicated to studying and making known the role of the Blessed Virgin Mary in the mystery of Christ and in the Church and in the history of salvation. Robert has served well as the past president of the society, and we have both given presentations at its annual meeting, held at various Marian shrines and retreat houses throughout the country, and have contributed to its publication, *Marian Studies.*

I have treasured our late-night discussions and always marvel at how much I learn from his reflections, bolstering my own knowledge of Mary garnered through study over the course of decades. Time and time again, I have found myself in awe of his ability to quote extemporaneously papal encyclicals on Mary and the writings of saints about the Mother of God, showing him to be among the most knowledgeable of Marian scholars in the Church today, while providing a glimpse into his own personal Marian devotion.

I have been grateful for Robert's consistent encouragement of my own research into the supernatural appearances and miracles of Mary throughout Christian history and the resulting Marian shrines and devotions that have developed worldwide. While not central to the Catholic faith, these blessed occasions of the Mother of God in our midst have changed human history and continue to draw us closer to her Son.

ws the trajectory of a Shalom World televi-
'ary, *Mother of All*, on which Robert and I
vith Dr. Mark Miravalle from Franciscan
ville and Dr. Carrie Gress, author of *The*
...ne series presented Marian scholars in a panel
...ssion format, reflecting on and debating various theological topics relevant to the study and understanding of Mary.

This book takes those discussions to a deeper level, exploring in greater detail the theological and historical context
of these prime examples of Marian intercession, structured
around her most significant titles. Each chapter contains two
parts.

In the first part, I delve into the history and cultural context
of each of ten Church-approved apparitions, enhancing the
stories with images that I've collected while traveling around
the world to produce my EWTN television series *The Miracle
Hunter.*

In the second part of each chapter, Robert delves into the
scriptures as well as two thousand years of Church teachings
to explain the significance of each title as well as its significance within the broader context of the Catholic faith. Readers
unfamiliar with these Marian events will be able to explore the
supernatural aspects of these apparitions while continuing to
learn from the systematic teachings of the Church, thereby
deepening their own understanding of the Catholic Church's
teachings about the Mother of God and growing in their own
devotion to her.

So come along with us and get to know a little better . . .
Mary: Virgin, Queen—and mother of us all!

CHAPTER 1

Mary as Blessed:
Our Lady of Knock

I beheld the three likenesses or figures . . . the Blessed
Virgin, St. Joseph, and St. John. . . . The eyes of the images
could be seen; they were like figures, inasmuch as they
did not speak. I was filled with wonder at the sight I saw;
I was so affected that I shed tears. I continued looking
on for fully an hour, and then I went away to visit Mrs.
Campbell, who was in a dying state. When we returned
the vision had disappeared.

DOMINICK BYRNE JR.
August 21, 1879[1]

There was no message of any kind given, no word was
uttered by any of the three celestial visitors. Yet the apparition must have a meaning, an extraordinary, deep, and
divine significance.

FR. WILLIAM J. SMITH[2]

Mary and Joseph rarely speak in scripture; instead,
they ponder the events unfolding in front of them
(see Luke 2:19, Matthew 1:20). Prayerfully and quietly,
Mary bore witness to the Incarnate Love that she brought into
the world by her fiat. Her blessedness is most clearly seen in

that simplicity and humility; no words are needed for God's glory to be revealed through her.

So it is with Knock. This singular apparition is sometimes referred to as "Our Lady of Silence," for none of the fifteen individuals who witnessed the appearance of the Blessed Mother heard her say a word. Rather, she stood silently with St. Joseph, St. John the Apostle, and the Lamb of God—standing with a people who had been ravaged over and over by famine, hunger, and disease. Why were they silent? We do not know. Perhaps they understood that their children simply needed them to bear witness to their suffering, and to encourage them to endure without losing hope—just as the Holy Family had persevered in faith and blessedness in raising the One who would bless us all.

Knock, Ireland, 1879

During a pouring rain on August 21, 1879, three human figures—the Virgin Mary, St. Joseph, and St. John the Evangelist (originally thought to be a bishop wearing a miter)—and a lamb on a plain altar with a cross appeared enveloped in a bright light over the gable of the village chapel in a small town in County Mayo, in western Ireland.

Fifteen witnesses, from the very young to the very old, experienced this silent apparition and stood in the rain for up to two hours while reciting the Rosary. When the occurrence began there was good light, but when it became very dark, witnesses could still see the figures very clearly since they appeared illuminated by a bright white light. The apparition did not flicker or move in any way, and unlike most famous Marian apparitions, there were no messages imparted.

The witnesses reported that the ground around the figures remained completely dry during the apparition although the wind was blowing from the south. Afterward, however, the ground at the gable became wet and the whole area dark.

This apparition occurred at a difficult and controversial time in Irish history. The social movements of that era challenged the landlord class. There was a significant conflict that caused the Land War (1879–1882), marked by civil disobedience by impoverished and exploited tenant farmers forcing wealthy landlords to sell their properties to the tenants, a situation that had been present for centuries in Ireland but that came to a head in that period. The government began to buy out the landlords and offer farmers mortgages to buy the land they worked, empowering them to become owners, rather than tenants.

A dilemma befell the Catholic Church, trying to support law and order and property rights while also espousing care and preferential treatment for the poor. The land movement and its violent demonstrations were loudly condemned initially by many priests, one of whom was Fr. Bartholomew Aloysius Cavanaugh, parish priest of Ballyhaunis, where the Knock apparition occurred, and later head of the investigative committee.

In June of 1879, a particularly aggressive demonstration contained by the police was targeted at him, as priests were expected to take the side of the poor. Many of the faithful may have seen the Knock apparition as a higher authority making a statement in support of better treatment of the poor.

The Witnesses

There were fifteen official eyewitnesses (three men, seven women, two teenage boys, and three children) including:

- Mrs. Margaret Byrne, sixty-eight: widow and mother of Mary, Margaret, Dominick Sr. and Patrick
- Mary Byrne, twenty-nine
- Dominick Byrne Sr., thirty-six: cousin of Dominick Jr.; uncle of Patrick Hill
- Margaret Byrne, twenty-one
- Dominick Byrne Jr., nineteen
- Patrick Byrne, sixteen

- Judith Campbell, twenty-two
- John Curry, five
- John Durkan, twenty-four
- Mrs. Hugh Flatley, forty-four
- Patrick Hill, eleven
- Mary McLoughlin, forty-five: housekeeper of the parish priest, Archdeacon Cavanaugh
- Catherine Murray, eight: niece of Margaret Byrne
- Bridget Trench, seventy-five
- Patrick Walsh, sixty-five

Why did God choose these particular individuals to receive this heavenly sign? It is unclear. While they were all living in this very poor village, these visionaries were not the most destitute people of the area. Several were related through the Byrne family, but others were outsiders with no real connection to the group.

The first person to see the vision was Mary McLoughlin, forty-five, the housekeeper of Archdeacon Cavanaugh, who lived three hundred yards away from the village chapel. She had gone to visit the neighbors but did not mention to them that she had detected something odd near the gable of the church. On the way back home, she was accompanied by Mary Byrne, whose job it was to close up the church for the night. The two called over a group of others when they began walking toward the light. Clusters of more and more people began to join. Then Mary McLoughlin ran to alert the priest and to try to get him to join the group, but he paid no attention.

Another group left the apparition still in progress to go fetch Mrs. Campbell, a neighbor woman thought to be dying, and her daughter, Mary. Five-year-old John Curry was the youngest of fifteen people who witnessed the apparition. He sat on Patrick Hill's shoulders as the group recited the Rosary as they watched the "beautiful things" for two hours in the pouring rain.

According to Mary Byrne:

> The Virgin stood erect, with eyes raised to heaven; her hands elevated to the shoulders or a little higher, the palms inclined slightly towards the shoulders or bosom; she wore a large cloak of a white color, hanging in full folds and somewhat loosely around her shoulders, and fastened to the neck. She wore a crown on the head, rather a large crown, and it appeared to me somewhat yellower than the dress or robes worn by Our Blessed Lady.[3]

Mary was described as "deep in prayer," with her eyes raised to heaven and her hands raised to the shoulders or a little higher, the palms inclined slightly to the shoulders. According to visionary Bridget Trench: "I went in immediately to kiss, as I thought, the feet of the Blessed Virgin; but I felt nothing in the embrace but the wall, and I wondered why I could not feel with my hands the figures which I had so plainly and so distinctly seen."[4]

The Investigation

Two commissions of inquiry (1879 and 1936) were established. The first investigative commission was set up within six weeks of the apparition on October 8, 1879, by Most Rev. Dr. John MacHale, archbishop of Tuam. It was comprised of Irish scholar and historian Canon Ulick Bourke as well as Canon James Waldron and Archdeacon Cavanaugh.

The fifteen witnesses were examined as well as a man who did not see the apparition close up but testified to seeing the illumination of the church from half a mile away at his farm. Depositions of witnesses were taken in the ensuing months, sometimes with all the panel members there and others to a partial panel. The commission looked at both the facts related to the apparition events and the miraculous cures that people were claiming. Among the considerations were whether the apparition emanated from natural causes and whether there was any proof positive of fraud. Neither a natural cause nor evidence of fraud were established.

The evidence recorded by the commission satisfied all the members and was deemed "trustworthy and satisfactory."[5] The details of this apparition were not publicized for several months in the local papers, but as soon as the commission's report was published, pilgrims began to flock to the site from all parts of the country and overseas, much to the dismay of the local priests, who actively discouraged attention given to the apparition events. Many sick were transported there and hundreds of cures were reported in the public press of that time, including the healing of two blind men shortly after the news of the apparition went public.

Beginning in 1880, pilgrims from all over Ireland were drawn to the Knock apparition site. In the span of a little more than a decade, however, the events had been largely forgotten or ignored except by the local community. In the 1930s, some people in Knock began to revive the devotion, perhaps partly due to the international attention given to Marian apparition sites at Lourdes and Fatima. These efforts were spearheaded by a married couple, William and Judy Coyne, who collected evidence from local people and encouraged the devotion with the help of a sympathetic bishop.

In 1936, Dr. Thomas Patrick Gilmartin, archbishop of Tuam, instituted a new investigative commission that again produced a positive verdict. All three surviving witnesses confirmed their original statements given in 1879. One of the witnesses was Mary O'Connell (née Byrne). She confirmed her testimony on her deathbed under oath, stating, "I am clear about everything I have said and I make this statement knowing I am about to go before my God." She died six weeks later.[6]

The verdict of the commission declared again that the "testimony of each of the fifteen official witnesses to the apparition was trustworthy and satisfactory." As a result of this revival of the devotion in the 1930s and the second commission inspired by that movement and interest, the current shrine and widespread Irish devotion to Our Lady of Knock exists. Now the only approved Marian apparition site in Ireland has become a destination for national and international pilgrimages.

Recognition from Rome

In addition to the positive verdict of two investigative commissions, the Vatican has also recognized the apparition at Knock.

On December 18, 1954, Our Lady of Knock was crowned with the same rites used by Pope Pius XII just a month earlier in Rome in the crowning of the miraculous, sixth-century Byzantine Marian icon *Salus Populi Romani*. Amid crowds of more than 450,000 people, Pope John Paul II visited the Knock shrine for the one hundredth anniversary of the apparition on September 30, 1979, and presented a Golden Rose, a seldom-bestowed token of papal honor and recognition, to the shrine.[7]

The feast of Our Lady of Knock is celebrated in Ireland and around the world on August 21.

Mary as "Blessed" in Scripture and throughout Church History

by Dr. Robert Fastiggi

In the 1879 apparition at Knock, Mary appeared along with St. Joseph, St. John the Apostle, an altar, and a lamb. For two hours she was visible to the onlookers, but she remained completely silent. Her mere presence was a blessing at Knock, and pilgrims have been blessed by her presence there since 1879. According to testimonies, the people's natural response was to pray the *Ave Maria*, crying out to the Blessed Mother for benediction.

This simple invocation, also known as the Hail Mary, is one of the best-known Marian prayers. The initial part of this prayer comes from the Gospel of Luke when Mary, pregnant with Jesus, sets out in haste to greet her kinswoman Elizabeth, who is pregnant with St. John the Baptist. Upon Mary's greeting, Elizabeth, filled with the Holy Spirit, cries out in a loud voice and says, "Most blessed are you among women, and blessed is the fruit of your womb" (Lk 1:42).

Here we see the principal reason why Mary is blessed: hers was the extraordinary privilege of carrying in her womb Jesus, the Incarnate Word of God. This is made clear from Elizabeth's next statement: "And how does this happen to me, that the mother of my Lord should come to me? For at the moment the sound of your greeting reached my ears, the infant in my womb leaped for joy" (Lk 1:43–44).

How does Mary's "blessedness" fulfill God's covenant promises to his people?

Elizabeth's words recall those spoken by King David when the ark of the covenant was brought to Jerusalem. When David sees the ark, he exclaims, "How can the ark of the LORD come to me?" (2 Sm 6:9). Mary is the living ark of the New Covenant because she is carrying the Lord Jesus, who is the foundation of the new and everlasting covenant between God and the human race.

In the Old Testament, God's people reverenced the ark as a sign of God's presence among them. We see one example of this in King David, who dances before the ark as he and the people shout with joy (see 2 Samuel 6:14–15). This same joy is clearly expressed by John the Baptist, who leaps in the womb of Elizabeth before Mary carrying the child Jesus (see Luke 1:44). This image of the ark is brought full circle in the book of Revelation, when the ark of God's covenant is seen within the heavenly temple (11:19), and Mary, "the woman clothed with the sun," appears (12:1).

In addition to becoming the mother of Jesus, why is Mary considered "blessed"?

In his 1987 encyclical, *Redemptoris Mater* (*Mother of the Redeemer*), Pope John Paul II offered another reason for Mary's blessedness: her great faith. Referring to the passage in scripture where Elizabeth tells Mary, "Blessed are you who believed that what was spoken to you by the Lord would be fulfilled" (Lk 1:45), the pope reflected deeply on Mary as the blessed one who believed. Speaking of Mary's obedience of faith at the Annunciation, the Holy Father wrote,

> Indeed, at the Annunciation Mary entrusted herself to God completely, with the "full submission of intellect and will," manifesting "the obedience of faith" to him who spoke to her through his messenger. She responded, therefore, with

all her human and feminine "I," and this response of faith included both perfect cooperation with "the grace of God that precedes and assists" and perfect openness to the action of the Holy Spirit, who "constantly brings faith to completion by his gifts." . . .

Mary uttered this fiat in faith. In faith she entrusted herself to God without reserve and "devoted herself totally as the handmaid of the Lord to the person and work of her Son." And as the Fathers of the Church teach—she conceived this Son in her mind before she conceived him in her womb: precisely in faith! Rightly therefore does Elizabeth praise Mary: "And blessed is she who believed that there would be a fulfillment of what was spoken to her from the Lord." These words have already been fulfilled: Mary of Nazareth presents herself at the threshold of Elizabeth and Zechariah's house as the Mother of the Son of God. This is Elizabeth's joyful discovery: "The mother of my Lord comes to me"! (*RM*, 13)

As Abraham was blessed by God because of his faith, so Mary is blessed because of hers. Pope John Paul II noted that "in the salvific economy of God's revelation, Abraham's faith constitutes the beginning of the Old Covenant; Mary's faith at the Annunciation inaugurates the New Covenant" (*RM*, 14). The *Catechism of the Catholic Church* points to the blessings that come to all the nations through the faith of Abraham and the faith of Mary: "Mary is 'blessed among women' because she believed in the fulfillment of the Lord's word. Abraham, because of his faith, became a blessing for all the nations of the earth. Mary, because of her faith, became the mother of believers, through whom all nations of the earth receive him who is God's own blessing: Jesus, the 'fruit of thy womb'" (*CCC*, 2676).

How is Mary, by virtue of her blessedness, a model for us?

Pope John Paul II also points to Mary as the blessed model of those who do the "will of God" (Mk 3:35). Some have understood Mark 3:31–35 as Jesus distancing himself from Mary because when he hears that Mary is with other members of his family asking for him, he says, "'Who are my mother and [my] brothers?' And looking around at those seated in the circle he said: 'Here are my mother and my brothers. For whoever does the will of God is my brother and sister and mother'" (Mk 3:33–35). In Luke 11:28, in a response to a woman from the crowd who cries out: "Blessed is the womb that carried you and the breasts at which you nursed" (Lk 11:27), Jesus, in a similar way, says, "Blessed are those who hear the word of God and observe it." Pope John Paul II offers this comment on these passages:

> Is Jesus thereby distancing himself from his mother according to the flesh? Does he perhaps wish to leave her in the hidden obscurity which she herself has chosen? If this seems to be the case from the tone of those words, one must nevertheless note that the new and different motherhood which Jesus speaks of to his disciples refers precisely to Mary in a very special way. Is not Mary the first of "those who hear the word of God and do it"? And therefore does not the blessing uttered by Jesus in response to the woman in the crowd refer primarily to her? Without any doubt, Mary is worthy of blessing by the very fact that she became the mother of Jesus according to the flesh ("Blessed is the womb that bore you, and the breasts that you sucked"), but also and especially because already at the Annunciation she accepted the word of God, because she believed it, because she was obedient to God, and because she "kept" the word and "pondered it in her heart" (cf. Lk. 1:38, 45; 2:19, 51) and by means of her whole life accomplished it. Thus we can say that the blessing proclaimed by Jesus is not in opposition, despite appearances, to the blessing uttered by the unknown woman, but rather coincides with that blessing in the person of this Virgin Mother, who called herself only "the handmaid of the Lord" (Lk. 1:38). If it is true that "all

generations will call her blessed" (cf. Lk. 1:48), then it can
be said that the unnamed woman was the first to confirm
unwittingly that prophetic phrase of Mary's Magnificat and
to begin the Magnificat of the ages. (*RM*, 20).

In her wonderful hymn, the Magnificat, Mary proclaims
that "from now on will all ages call me blessed" (Lk 1:48). She
recognizes, though, that it is God who has blessed her when she
says: "The Mighty One has done great things for me, and holy
is his name" (Lk 1:49). God blesses Mary, but he also blesses
humanity through her just as he blessed the nations through
Abraham (cf. Gn 12:3).

*What is the connection between Mary's blessedness and her
life of virtue?*

Mary embodies all of the Beatitudes taught by her divine Son
in his Sermon on the Mount (see Matthew 5:3–10): She is poor
in spirit, and she knows what it is to mourn. She is meek, and
she hungers and thirsts for the righteousness of all her spiritual
children. She is merciful because she is "the Mother of mercy."
She is clean of heart because her heart is all-pure and free from
sinful desire. Similarly, those who follow the Beatitudes are
blessed by God.

As the Queen of Peace, Mary is a peacemaker by her constant intercession for her children on Earth. We see this even in
her silence at Knock, where she and St. Joseph wordlessly interceded for the community that had suffered so much through
famine and want. Whenever her children suffer, Mary intercedes, just as she shared in the suffering of her crucified Son,
who was persecuted for the sake of righteousness. In a very
real sense, Mary is the woman of the Beatitudes who has been
blessed mightily by God.

How is it possible for us to imitate Mary, both in blessing and being blessed?

To be blessed by God is to receive his favor, but "blessed" is also used in the liturgical and prayer life of the Church as a way of giving honor, praise, or reverence.[8] This liturgical use is rooted in scripture. In praying the Psalms, we bless the Lord with all our being and bless his holy name (see Psalm 103:1). During the preparation of the gifts at Mass, we repeat the response: "Blessed be God forever."

In the prayer life of the Church, many blessings are likewise called upon the Virgin Mary. The Divine Praises recited after Benediction of the Blessed Sacrament include praises of Mary as blessed: "Blessed be the great Mother of God, Mary most holy. Blessed be her holy and immaculate conception. Blessed be her glorious assumption. Blessed be the Name of Mary, Virgin and Mother."[9]

Is this idea of Mary as the Blessed One a relatively recent development in Church teaching?

Not at all. Early in the twentieth century, the Greek text of an ancient prayer dating back to the third or fourth century was discovered in Egypt. This prayer is called the *Sub tuum praesidium* because the Latin version—known since the Middle Ages—begins: "Under thy protection we take refuge" (*Sub tuum praesidium confugimus*). Translated from Greek, the prayer reads: "Beneath your compassion, we take refuge, O Mother of God. Do not despise our petitions in time of trouble, but rescue us from dangers, only pure, only blessed one (*móne Aguń móne eúlogeméne*)."

The Latin translation of this ancient Marian prayer also recognizes Mary as blessed. It reads: "Under thy protection, we take refuge O Holy Mother of God; do not despise our petitions in our necessities, but deliver us always from all dangers, O Glorious and Blessed Virgin (*Virgo gloriosa et benedicta*). Amen."

Mary is likewise recognized as blessed by Church Fathers, saints, and popes throughout Church history. St. Ephrem the Syrian (ca. 306–373) compared Mary to the blessed city of Bethlehem when he wrote: "Blessed are you, Bethlehem, whom fortified towns and fortified cities envied. . . . Blessed is the girl He found worthy to indwell, and also the town He found worthy to inhabit."[10] Because Mary is recognized as "most blessed" among women in scripture (Lk 1:42), it is only fitting that the word "blessed" be ever connected to her name. She is indeed the "Blessed Mother" and the "Blessed Virgin Mary," and she will be blessed forever.

◇◇

PRAYER TO OUR LADY OF KNOCK ⚜

Our Lady of Knock, Queen of Ireland, you gave hope to your people in a time of distress and comforted them in sorrow. You have inspired countless pilgrims to pray with confidence to your divine Son, remembering his promise, "Ask and you shall receive, seek and you shall find."

Help me to remember that we are all pilgrims on the road to heaven. Fill me with love and concern for my brothers and sisters in Christ, especially those who live with me. Comfort me when I am sick, lonely, or depressed. Teach me how to take part ever more reverently in the Holy Mass. Give me a greater love of Jesus in the Blessed Sacrament. Pray for me now and at the hour of my death. Amen.[11]

CHAPTER 2

Mary as Virgin:
Our Lady of Guadalupe

Have no fear, for I am the Mother of God, by whom the
human race received redemption. Go to your home and
tell the clergy and other people to come to this place . . .
and dig here, where they will find a statue.

> BLESSED VIRGIN MARY to the cowherd Gil Cordero
> Cáceres, Extremadura, Spain, 1326

I am the ever-virgin Holy Mary, Mother of the True God
for whom we live.

> BLESSED VIRGIN MARY to Juan Diego
> Tepeyac Hill, Mexico, December 1531

Many Catholics are familiar with the story of Juan Diego
and Our Lady of Guadalupe, who appeared to him
at Tepeyac Hill, and caused roses to bloom mysteriously, out of season, and imprint a miraculous image when
gathered inside his tilma. But did you know that veneration
to Our Lady of Guadalupe can be traced back even further, to
a statue thought to be carved by St. Luke the Evangelist? The
two faces we have of Our Lady of Guadalupe appear to be
very different—one a wooden statue clad in regal garments,
the other a miraculous image imprinted on an ancient cape of

cactus fiber. And yet they speak of the same threefold reality
of Our Lady as Virgin, Mother, and Queen.

In this chapter we will focus on the first of these appella-
tions, Mary as the young virgin who miraculously conceived
and gave birth to the Redeemer of the World while retaining
her virginal purity. The perpetual virginity of Mary—the article of Catholic dogma that states that Mary remained a virgin throughout her life, before, during, and after the birth of
Christ—is a teaching that confounds many Christians. How
is it possible that this teenage girl, married to Joseph, would
have remained a virgin after giving birth to Christ? And yet,
this article of Catholic belief is found in the earliest creeds of
the Church, affirming that Jesus was "born of the Virgin Mary."[1]

Why would her virginity be such an important sign of
God's revelation that, fifteen centuries after the birth of Christ,
Our Lady of Guadalupe would appear to Juan Diego clad in the
tunic of an unmarried girl, the girdle around her waist being a
sign of her virginity yet the high position of the bow indicating
that she is with child? Stay with us as we take a closer look at
these questions, so that you might ponder in a new and fresh
way the unique role of the Blessed Virgin Mary in the salvation
story and come to an even better understanding of how her
maternal heart remains pure and undivided today as she leads
her children to her beloved Son.

Mexico City, Mexico, 1531

One of the most significant Marian devotions in Catholicism,
Our Lady of Guadalupe, is honored at the Basilica de Nuestra
Señora de Guadalupe, north of Mexico City. It is a place that
has been visited by several popes as well as millions of people
every year. Her feast day is set as an optional memorial on
the general Roman calendar, and Pope John Paul II canonized
visionary Juan Diego in 2002. For all these reasons and more,
Our Lady of Guadalupe stands out as one of the most highly
recognized and celebrated of all Marian apparitions.

The ubiquitous Guadalupan image is one of the most widely reproduced portraits of any woman in world history. And yet most Catholics do not realize that the Blessed Mother had appeared in this form at least once before, more than two centuries previously and an ocean's distance away.

According to pious legend, in 1326 the Virgin Mary appeared in Cáceres, a province of Extremadura, Spain, to a cowherd named Gil Cordero as he searched for a lost cow. The Virgin led him to a mound of stones on which he saw his cow lying motionless, as if dead. Cordero was ready to cut off its hide when the cow awoke. Mary told Cordero to dig at the spot, and he enlisted the help of local authorities to excavate the area, revealing a cave that contained a statue with an ancient document explaining its origin: It was a famous wonder-working statue that Pope Gregory the Great had sent to Spain nearly eight hundred years earlier. A church and later a basilica were built, helping to make the devotion to Our Lady of Guadalupe one of the most popular in all of Spain and a favorite Marian title of Christopher Columbus, who dedicated an island he discovered (Guadeloupe) to her patronage.

The Statue of Our Lady of Guadalupe from Extremadura, Spain.

How are these two events connected? In truth, it is unclear precisely how the name "Our Lady of Guadalupe" came to be associated with the apparitions in Mexico, whether it was the name picked up by the Spanish upon hearing the native account or whether it was the name given by Our Lady herself to Juan Diego's uncle, Juan Bernardino. The *Nican Mopohua* (the account in Nahuatl, an indigenous language) that is revered as the foundation of the apparition's tradition, supports the latter explanation.[2] Other scholars contend that the visionary St. Juan Diego called her *Tequatlanipeuh*, meaning "that which originated on the peak of crags" in his native Nahuatl; to the Spanish ear, that sounded like Guadalupe, an already familiar name due to Our Lady of Guadalupe in Extremadura, Spain.[3]

As she did in Spain, the Virgin Mary appeared to a simple worker with the love of a mother for a singular individual, but her appearance made a lasting impact on an entire nation. In December 1531, the Blessed Mother appeared four times on Tepeyac Hill to Juan Diego (1474–1548), an indigenous Mexican convert to Christianity. Juan Diego was born with the name "Cuauhtlatoatzin" ("the talking eagle") in Cuautlitlán, which is today part of Mexico City. He was a gifted member of the Chichimeca people, a nomadic people living in the Anáhuac, a valley region. When Juan Diego was fifty years old, he was baptized by a Franciscan priest, Fr. Peter da Gand, one of the first Franciscan missionaries.

When the Virgin appeared to Juan Diego, she requested that a temple be built there in order to honor her Son. When the poor peasant was dubious about getting the bishop to listen to him, she comforted Juan:

> Am I not here, I, who am your mother? Are you not under
> my shadow and protection? Am I not your fountain of life?
> Are you not in the folds of my mantle? . . . Is there anything
> else you need?[4]

Juan Diego's persistence in attempting to persuade the Spanish bishop-elect in Mexico to begin this great undertaking was received favorably only when, during an audience, the devout native unfurled his tilma (cloak), from which fell dozens of Castilian roses blooming out of season in winter. The garment itself was miraculously emblazoned with an image of the Mother of God robed in native garb.

In this image, the Virgin has dark skin and hair, leading to her being called *la morenita* ("the dark little one"), allowing the indigenous people to see her as one of their own. She is wearing a maternity belt to indicate that she is pregnant, and on her stomach is a glyph: the *nahui ollin*, a four-petaled flower indicating north, south, east, and west, or God in his omnipresence. Although every other glyph is repeated on her dress, this one is unique from any of the other arabesque designs in the image, pointing to her unique identity as the Virgin Mother of God.

The History of the Tilma

While the tilma itself still exists and has been subjected to scientific testing, the documentation surrounding these visions is limited, and the visionary himself, despite being canonized by Pope John Paul II in 2002, does not have much conclusively written about him. In the first formal inquiry and investigation, named *Informaciones Guadalupana*, from February 18 to March 22, 1666, Juan Diego was called a "holy man." A great oral tradition surrounds these apparition events and supplies enough details to assure us of their veracity.

Some have suggested that the image contains embedded symbolic meanings for both the natives and Spaniards who have encountered it, acting as a catechetical device. To the eyes and understanding of the people of this region at that time, the tilma reads as a *codex*, a collection of Nahuatl symbols and glyphs on the inside robe that would serve as a teaching tool.

Our Lady's pose, standing in front of the rays of the sun and on top of the moon and with the stars to her back on her mantle, suggests that she is greater than these celestial bodies, which were divine personages for the Aztec people. However, the eyes of the image are downcast and the head bowed, indicating that the woman is not divine herself. Rather, she stands humbly, her hands in a prayerful posture before God. Even her feet are said by some to be in movement, portraying her as dancing in prayer.

The wondrous image on Juan Diego's cactus-fiber cloak, inspiring the construction of these magnificent places of worship, should have decayed within decades, but remains to this day. Numerous copies have been made over the years to try to match the image's beauty and simulate its preservation. In the famous Battle of Lepanto in 1571, Christian forces overcame great odds and the formidable Turkish fleet with all of Europe praying the Rosary and Admiral Giovanni Andrea Doria sailing with a copy of the miraculous image of Our Lady of Guadalupe in his ship's stateroom. Another copy of the image was created in 1789, painted on a similar coarse-fiber surface and placed in glass next to the tilma. It lasted eight years before the heat and environmental conditions caused it to be taken down due to the fading of its colors and fraying of its threads.

Scientific Examination

Adolfo Orozco, a researcher and physicist at the National University of Mexico, sees no explanation for how the original tilma remained intact despite having been "exposed for approximately 116 years without any kind of protection, receiving all the infrared and ultraviolet radiation from the tens of thousands of candles near it and exposed to the humid and salty air around the temple."[5]

The tilma has survived more than the ravages of Mexico's heat and humidity and the smoke of votive candles. In 1785, a worker accidentally spilled nitric acid solution onto a large portion of the image while cleaning the frame. It should have been eaten away almost immediately, but the image remains in good condition. In 1921, an anti-Church activist placed dynamite in a rose display at the altar of the Basilica of Our Lady of Guadalupe. When the explosion went off, the marble of the altar and floor were destroyed and the nearby metal crucifix was mangled, but the image itself stayed intact.

The tilma belongs to a rare group of miraculous images classified as *acheiropoeita* (Greek, "not made from human hands"). One of the great mysteries of the Guadalupan image is how it was created. The image on the tilma is composed of pigments that have not been identified by chemical analysis as the product of animal, vegetable, or mineral dye. No underdrawing has been identified below the painting.

On May 7, 1979, Philip Serna Callahan, an accomplished biologist and author of numerous scientific books and papers, was invited to conduct infrared photographic tests on the tilma. He determined that portions of the face, hands, robe, and mantle had been painted in one step, with no sketches or corrections and no visible brush strokes:

> In terms of this infrared study, there is no way to explain either the kind of color pigments or the maintenance of color luminosity and brightness over the centuries. When consideration is given to the fact that there is no under drawing, sizing or over varnish, and the weave of the fabric itself is utilized to give the portrait depth, no explanation of the portrait is possible by infrared techniques. It is remarkable that after more than four centuries there is no fading or cracking of the original figure on any portion of the agave tilma, which should have deteriorated centuries ago.[6]

Study of the tilma by scientists and others has rendered some noteworthy claims including musical notes corresponding to the tilma's glyphs that comprise a composition and a topographical map with the glyphs for water and mountains aligning with Mexican geography. Others have purported such oddities (without scientific validation) as a heartbeat detected and a consistent temperature of a human-like 98.6 degrees Fahrenheit.

In 1956, ophthalmologist Dr. Javier Torroella Bueno identified in the eyes of the image a triple reflection (called the Samson-Purkinje effect) characteristic of all human eyes and reported that the distortion of the images agrees with the curvature of the cornea. Additional noteworthy analysis was done in 1981 by Peruvian engineer Dr. José Aste Tönsmann, who published a study of high-resolution imaging used to magnify the image 2,500 times, brightening it at 25,000 illuminated points per square millimeter, and running noise-reduction filters to enhance the image. This examination revealed an image of thirteen people in the pupils and corneas of the eyes of the Virgin on the tilma, and their appearance is consistent with the moment of the story when Juan Diego revealed the image to the bishop-elect and his attendants. Dr. Tönsmann published his findings in 1998 in a book titled *El secreto de sus ojos: Estudio digital de las imágenes reflejadas en los ojos de la Virgen de Guadalupe* ("The Secret of Her Eyes").

Also noteworthy were the studies done on December 22, 1981, at the Observatory Laplace in Mexico City, in which Fr. Mario Rojas Sánchez and Dr. Juan Homero Hernández Illescas analyzed the stellar arrangement that appears on the mantle of the Virgin. They concluded that the stars were consistent with what astronomers believe was in the sky above Mexico City on the day the apparition occurred—in the winter-morning solstice of December 12, 1531, Saturday, at 10:26 a.m.

The miracles and mysteries of the tilma have fascinated believers and inspired scientific exploration in an effort to understand this image for centuries. But the tilma of Our Lady of Guadalupe, in standing as a symbol of God's enduring love, reminds us of Our Lady's call to St. Juan Diego for evangelization. At a time when many Catholics throughout Europe lost their way during the Protestant Reformation, nine million Aztecs were drawn to the Catholic faith in the decade following the visions of Mary.

Our Lady of Guadalupe: Patroness of the Americas

As Our Lady requested, a chapel was indeed built on the hill, where previously had been a sacred site devoted to a temple for the Aztec goddess Tonantzin Coatlaxopeuh, destroyed by the Spanish settlers. With the bishop's permission, Juan Diego lived the rest of his life as a hermit in a small hut near the chapel where the miraculous image was placed for veneration. Here he cared for the church and the first pilgrims who came to pray to the Mother of Jesus. That first church was replaced by newer ones named for Our Lady of Guadalupe in 1622 and 1709; the new basilica was completed in 1976.

By honoring her under the title "Patroness of the Americas," the Catholic Church recognizes Mary's importance as a maternal presence and symbol of hope to Catholics in Mexico and around the world. In his historic 1979 visit to the Basilica of Our Lady of Guadalupe in Mexico City, Pope John Paul II called her a "Star of Evangelization," knelt before her image, invoked her motherly assistance, and called upon her as Mother of the Americas.

Several other popes have also drawn attention to Mary under the title of Our Lady of Guadalupe. In his 1754 papal bull *Non Est Equidem,* Pope Benedict XIV declared Our Lady of Guadalupe "Patroness of New Spain."[7] Pope Leo XIII authorized the canonical coronation of the image in October 1895. She has been declared Patroness of Latin America (by Pope Pius X in 1910), Patroness of the Philippines (by Pope Pius XI in 1935), and Patroness of the Americas (by Pope Pius XII in 1946); she was later invoked as Mother of the Americas by Pope John XXIII in 1961. Pope Paul VI gave the image its first Golden Rose in 1966, and Pope Francis granted that the image of a Golden Rose be presented at the basilica on November 18, 2013, before bringing a gold-plated silver crown for the image with the inscription *"Mater Mea, Spes Mea"* ("My Mother, My Hope") during his apostolic visit to the basilica in February 2016.

With a colorful history replete with a saintly visionary, miracles, scientific exploration, and the full support of the Church, Our Lady of Guadalupe has been an inspiration for the Mexican people and the millions of pilgrims who visit her, even traversing the plaza in devotion on their knees to honor the Mother of God. Believers see Mary under this title as truly their mother, as did Pope Francis during his 2016 visit when he remarked, "Like Juan Diego, we know that here is our mother, we know that we are under her shadow and her protection, which is the source of our joy." Although Our Lady appeared to St. Juan Diego almost five hundred years ago, her maternal protection and call to evangelization draw us closer to her Son even in our lives today.

Mary as "Virgin" in Scripture and throughout Church History
by Dr. Robert Fastiggi

As soon as Catholics hear the name of Mary, we immediately identify her as "the Blessed Virgin Mary." Why is Mary's virginity so important? And why is it necessary to believe that Mary remained a virgin *ante-partum* (before giving birth), *in partu* (in childbirth), and perpetually *post-partum* (after giving birth)? We will explore this in greater detail later in this chapter. But first, let us consider what the scriptures have to say about this aspect of Mary's role in salvation history and her identity as the "ever-virgin" mother of Christ.

Did Mary have other children besides Jesus?

This question often leads to disagreements between Catholics and other Christians. It is usually thought that the belief in Mary's perpetual virginity is something only Catholics hold, and therefore, all other Christians believe that Mary and Joseph had other children via marital relations after the virginal birth of Jesus. Actually, belief in Mary's perpetual virginity is not only a dogma for Catholics but for Eastern Orthodox as well.[8] It is also worth noting that the most prominent early Protestant writers (e.g., Luther, Zwingli, and Calvin) likewise believed that Mary did not have any other children besides Jesus.[9]

Why does the Bible speak of Jesus' "brothers and sisters"?

The Bible does speak about brothers and sisters of Jesus, but it never specifies that any of these are also children of Mary, the mother of Jesus. Of the four brothers listed by name—James, Joseph (called Joses in Mark), Judas, and Simon (see Matthew 13:55 and Mark 6:3)—two of them (James and Joseph) are specifically mentioned as being sons of another Mary (see Matthew 27:56).

All the other texts referring to Jesus' "brothers" either use the singular Greek word for brothers (*adelphos*) or the plural *adelphoi*, which could mean brothers (gender specific), brethren, or brothers and sisters.[10] "Brothers" could also be used to refer to close relatives or those with whom one has a special bond.[11]

James and Joseph are specifically identified as being sons of another Mary (see Matthew 27:56), possibly the wife of Clopas, who looked upon Jesus' Crucifixion "from a distance" with Jesus' mother (Mt 27:56; see also John 19:25).[12] Because of this, we can't say for sure the specific relation between James and Joseph, the "brothers" of the Lord, and Jesus. One ancient tradition holds that Clopas was the brother of St. Joseph; thus, his wife (the "other Mary"), would actually have been the sister-in-law of Jesus' mother and the legal cousins (or "brothers") of the Lord.

Although the Greek word for cousin (*anepsios*) is different from the Greek word for brother (*adelphos*), the language spoken by Jesus and his family was Aramaic. In Hebrew (which is similar to Aramaic) the word for brother (*'ah*) can mean close relative as well as blood brother, as we find in the story of Abram and Lot in Genesis 14.[13]

Even in the New Testament, the words "brother" and "brothers" (*adelphos* and *adelphoi*) are used in a variety of senses. In 1 Corinthians 5:11, Paul speaks of a Christian as one who is called "brother" (*adelphos*). In 1 Corinthians 15:6, Paul reports that the risen Lord was seen by five hundred "brothers" (*adelphoi*) at once. He also addresses his letter to the Colossians "to the holy ones and faithful brothers [*adelphoi*] in Christ" (Col 1:2). Surely they weren't all his blood brothers!

If Mary remained a virgin throughout her life, why is Jesus referred to as Mary's "firstborn son" in Luke 2:7? Does not the word "until" in Matthew 1:25 suggest that Mary and Joseph had normal marital relations after Jesus' birth (and therefore likely had other children)?

In Luke 2:7, the Greek term *"prototokos"* (firstborn male child) had special significance for the Hebrews;[14] it had nothing to do with whether the woman had other children.

Similarly, the biblical use of "until" in Matthew 1:25 indicates a period of time up to a certain event. It does not necessarily suggest that a certain action takes place after this period of time is complete. For example, we are told that "Saul's daughter Michal was childless until her death" (2 Sm 6:23, NAB). Certainly, she did not have children after her death![15]

Are there passages in the Bible that support Mary's perpetual virginity?

Yes. When Mary is told by the angel that she will conceive and bear a son, she asks: "How can this be, since I have no relations with a man?" (Lk 1:34). This would be a strange reply coming from a betrothed girl unless she had made a previous promise of virginity. If Mary had younger children, born after Jesus, how was she able to go each year to Jerusalem for the feast of Passover (see Luke 2:41) along with Joseph and Jesus? We also might ask why the other children were not mentioned as being part of this pilgrimage. Finally, from the Cross in John 19:27, Jesus entrusted the care of his mother to the beloved disciple (by tradition, John, the son of Zebedee). If Jesus had blood brothers still alive, would it not have been proper for them to be Mary's caretakers?

In the early Church, St. Jerome (340–420) and others also understood Song of Songs 4:12 as a prophecy of Mary's perpetual virginity: "A garden enclosed, my sister, my bride, a garden enclosed, a fountain sealed."

Was belief in Mary's perpetual virginity widespread in the early Church?

Yes. The Yale historian Jaroslav Pelikan noted that the "vast majority" of early Christians believed Mary to be "ever-virgin."[16] Church Fathers such as St. Augustine and St. Gregory of Nyssa believed that Mary, as a girl, made a vow of perpetual virginity. According to the Proto-Gospel of James, Mary married Joseph, an older widower who had children from his first marriage. Even though this gospel is not included in the New Testament canon, it reveals a very early concern with Mary's virginity and the explanation of Jesus' "brothers and sisters" as children of Joseph from his previous marriage. Reference to Mary as "ever-virgin" is found in many writings of the Church Fathers, and she was given this title at the Second Council of Constantinople in 553.

Early Christian writers such as Clement of Alexandria (ca. 150–215) and Origen (185–254) believed that Mary remained ever-virgin, as did all the great Doctors of the Church of the fourth century: St. Ambrose (339–397), St. Augustine (354–430), St. Jerome (ca. 347–420), St. Athanasius (ca. 295–373), and St. Basil the Great (ca. 330–379).

The Lateran Synod of 649, presided over by Pope Martin I, taught that Mary gave birth to Jesus "without corruption, her virginity remaining equally inviolate after his birth."[17] Fr. Juan Luis Bastero believed this teaching has the dogmatic value of an *ex cathedra* papal definition because the synod "was presided over and sanctioned by the Pope, who proposed this doctrine as a condition for being in communion with the Roman See and condemned its denial with an anathema."[18] Vatican II likewise taught that, in giving birth, Mary's virginity was not diminished but sanctified.[19]

In his May 24, 1992, discourse in Capua, Italy, in honor of the sixteenth centenary of the 392 Council of Capua, Pope John Paul II drew a parallel between the begetting of Christ *ex intacta Virgine* (from the intact Virgin) and his Resurrection *ex intacto sepulcro* (from the intact sepulcher).[20]

As noted above, Mary is spoken of as "ever-virgin" in the liturgy (cf. the penitential prayer and the first Eucharistic canon). The title "ever-virgin" was attributed to Mary at the Second Council of Constantinople (553), the local Lateran Council under Pope Martin I (649), and the Profession of Faith of the Council of Trent (1564). In his solemn definition of the Assumption of 1950, Pope Pius XII refered to Mary as "the Immaculate Mother of God, Mary ever-virgin" (*Immaculatam Deiparam semper Virginem Mariam*). The perpetual virginity of Mary is a solemn *de fide* dogma of the Catholic faith by reason of the ordinary universal Magisterium of the Church. It also finds support in the extraordinary Magisterium—ecumenical councils and *ex cathedra* papal pronouncements.

How would you summarize the key theological insights about Mary's perpetual virginity, throughout the history of the Church?

Here are twelve theological insights as to why Mary's perpetual virginity has always been a core Marian dogma throughout the history of the Church.

1. Clement of Alexandria (d. 215): Mary is a model of the Church, which is herself virgin and mother.[21]
2. St. Basil of Caesarea (d. 379): Confirms her virginity at the time when she conceived Jesus; St. Joseph was witness to Mary's perpetual virginity as protection against detractors who denied her virginity.[22]
3. St. Gregory Nazianzen (d. 390): Mary is the Spouse of God. Her perpetual virginity manifests her spousal love and fidelity to God.[23]
4. St. Gregory of Nyssa (d. 394): That Mary had taken a vow of virginity is suggested by Luke 1:34.[24]
5. St. Ambrose (d. 397): Mary is the model of virgins.[25]
6. St. Epiphanius (d. 403): Mary has always been spoken of as "the Virgin Mary," which would make no sense if she lost her virginity.[26]
7. St. John Chrysostom (d. 407): Jesus entrusted the care of his mother to the beloved disciple, John, from the Cross in John 19:26–27.[27]
8. St. Jerome (d. 419): Mary's virginal womb was the shrine of the Holy Spirit, so it was unbecoming and presumptuous for any man to defile this shrine.[28]
9. Caelius Sedulius (d. ca. 440–450)[29] and St. Jerome[30]: Mary's virginity must be perpetual because "this gate must remain closed. . . . Because the LORD, the God of Israel, came through it" (Ez 44:2).
10. St. Thomas Aquinas (d. 1274): Just as Christ is the only-begotten Son of the Father, so it was fitting that Christ be the only-begotten Son of his mother. [31]
11. Furthermore, according to Aquinas, it would be ungrateful for Mary to forfeit her virginity, which had been miraculously preserved by God. It would show that Mary was not content with Jesus as her Son.[32]

31

tium holds that Mary's perpetual virginity shows
ommitment to God, and she becomes a model of
l and detached life" (*LG*, 46).

The recognition of Mary's perpetual virginity has been the
constant and traditional teaching of the Church. We honor and
love the ever-virgin Mary as the model of consecrated virginity
and the model of all mothers because she is the Mother of the
Word Incarnate.

◇◇◇

JOHN PAUL II'S PRAYER TO OUR LADY OF GUADALUPE ⚜

Virgin of Guadalupe, Mother of the Americas . . .
Grant to our homes the grace of loving and respecting
life in its beginnings, with the same love with which you
conceived in your womb the life of the Son of God.

Blessed Virgin Mary, protect our families, so that they may
always be united, and bless the upbringing of our children. . . .
We beg you grant us a great love for all the holy Sacraments, which
are, as it were, the signs that your Son left us on earth.

Thus, Most Holy Mother, with the peace of God in our
conscience, with our hearts free from evil and hatred, we will
be able to bring to all true joy and true peace, which come to us
from your Son, Our Lord Jesus Christ, who with God the Father
and the Holy Spirit, lives and reigns forever and ever. Amen.[33]

CHAPTER 3

Mary as Mother of God: Our Lady of Kibeho

My child, I love you. Never be afraid of me, in fact, play with me! I love children who will play with me because it shows me their love and trust. . . . You should never be afraid of me; you should always love me as I love you.

OUR LADY OF KIBEHO to Alphonsine
November 29, 1981[1]

"I see a river of blood! What does that mean? . . ." the seer cried out, as the Holy Mother revealed one horrifying vision after another. . . . The Blessed Mother was warning the crowd gathered in front of the visionary of the horror that awaited Rwanda.

IMMACULÉE ILIBAGIZA,
Our Lady of Kibeho [2]

The gentle face, large brown eyes, and folded hands of the "Mother of the Word" gazes down from her pedestal in what was once a dormitory room, just a few steps from the large sanctuary where thousands gather to pray at the Shrine of Our Lady of Kibeho in southern Rwanda. Inside the church, she holds up her hands as a gentle reminder to her children to be at peace with one another, and to stay close.

35

When the Mother of the Word first appeared to three Rwandan schoolgirls and gave them her message of warning, no one listened, and in 1994, a devastating period of bloodshed and violence swept across the country in what became known as the Rwandan genocide; one million Tutsi and moderate Hutus were killed in just one hundred days. Witnesses such as Immaculée Ilibagiza and Fr. Ubald Rugirangoga,[3] who survived the carnage, have worked to bring peace back to their homeland, where today the Mother of the Word is remembered as a sign of hope.

It is partly our fallen human nature, it seems, that we become so easily divided by the things that ought to unite us, as Jesus predicted in the Gospel of Matthew: "You will hear of wars and reports of wars; see that you are not alarmed, for these things must happen, but it will not yet be the end" (Mt 24:5–6). It is into this reality that the Mother of God appears, alternately warning us of the reality of evil and reassuring us of the abundant mercies that are available to those who love Jesus enough to pick up their cross, as did Mary's Son, and follow him all the way home.

Kibeho, Rwanda, 1981

Rwanda, known as the "land of a thousand hills," is a central African country that has been a hotbed of violence since it achieved independence from Belgium in 1962. The minority ethnic group, the Tutsi, once favored by the colonialists, represented an intolerable threat to the majority Hutu government. Every few years, localized attacks on Tutsi populations occurred to hold the balance of power in check. But ultimately, it was decided the only sure way to peace was genocide, and a systematic plan was laid out to kill every Tutsi man, woman, and child along with every moderate Hutu who resisted.

In 1981, the Virgin Mary appeared to three young students on a hillside in Kibeho in southern Rwanda. Six girls and one boy claimed to see the Mother of God and her divine Son. In the end, only three of them—seventeen-year-old Alphonsine Mumureke, twenty-year-old Nathalie Mukamazimpaka, and twenty-one-year-old Marie Claire Mukangango—received the local bishop's solemn approval.

According to the seers, a beautiful woman appeared to them and asked the people to convert their hearts and change their lives, predicting a great tragedy with "rivers of blood." Throughout these apparitions, Mary asked the children to prepare the world for the return of her Son with messages calling for prayer, fasting, and conversion. The local bishop found the visions authentic, saying that "there are more reasons to believe in the apparitions than to deny them."[4] It is not uncommon for some Marian apparitions to be associated with prophetic words and predictions of the future. This was certainly a dramatic example, in light of what transpired in the following years.

How Did It All Begin?

On November 28, 1981, Alphonsine told her teachers and classmates that she had seen the Mother of God during lunch in the dining room of their girls' boarding school. When she had asked the identity of the woman, she received a reply in Kinyarwanda: "I am the *Nyina wa Jambo* [Mother of the Word]. I have come to calm you because I have heard your prayers. I would like your friends to have faith, because they do not believe strongly enough."[5]

The Virgin explained to her that "Mother of the Word" is synonymous with *Umubyeyl W'iamna*, "Mother of God."[6] With this most important Marian title, the Virgin reminded Alphonsine of her most blessed and unique role in salvation history.

When Alphonsine's initial reports were ridiculed, most notably by future visionary Marie Claire (who called her a "fool"), the young visionary prayed that other children might see the Mother of the Word as well. In January of 1982, the Virgin began appearing to Nathalie, and these visions continued for nearly two years. On March 2, 1982, Our Lady began appearing to Marie Claire, and those visions continued for six months.

Alphonsine described Mary's appearance in these visions in this way: She was about twenty-five years old, wearing a blue veil and "a seamless white dress and also a white veil on her head . . . her hands were clasped together on her breast, and her fingers pointed to the sky. . . . I could not determine the color of her skin but she was of incomparable beauty."[7]

The apparitions were very different from those experienced at the most widely known approved sites of Marian visions, with the experiences often lasting for several hours. Alphonsine's emotions were visibly on display with dramatic tears and laughter in response to the Virgin's words, and she would sometimes faint from exhaustion when it was over. On August 15, 1982, on the Solemnity of the Assumption, the Virgin appeared weeping with a message that terrified Alphonsine so greatly that she fell to the ground, begging not to see the ghastly images any longer.

Local devotion quickly grew. Many held prayer meetings and pilgrimages, and miracles were reported, such as conversions, healings, and abnormal solar phenomena: the sun appeared to pulsate, spin, or split in two—something that was said to be reminiscent of the famed October 13, 1917, "Miracle of the Sun" at Fatima.

These long-running apparitions (Alphonsine's visions ended on November 28, 1989, exactly eight years to the day of Mary's first appearance to her) are now considered an authentic prophecy of the ethnic genocide that would take place in the country thirteen years later. Although Catholics comprised at least 65 percent of the population at that time, more than a million lives were lost in the genocide, often at the hands of former friends, neighbors, and even fellow parishioners. Marie Claire, who continued to receive visions until September 15, 1982, was one of the genocide victims at Kibeho. Nathalie escaped to the Democratic Republic of the Congo and then to Kenya. Alphonsine entered religious life in Italy.[8]

The Investigation

In March 1982, a medical commission began to investigate the reports, led by Dr. Venant Ntabomvura, an ear, nose, and throat specialist. Some time later, a theological commission was appointed as well. Public devotion to Our Lady of Kibeho was authorized on August 15, 1988, by the bishop of the diocese.

At a solemn Mass celebrated on June 29, 2001, Bishop Augustin Misago of Gikongoro officially declared the visions to be authentic: "Yes, the Virgin Mary did appear in Kibeho on November 28, 1981," and over the "course of the following six months."[9] He could not, however, confirm the veracity of all the people who reported apparitions; the visions claimed by Stephanie Mukamurenzi and Agnes Kamagaju, for example, were rejected. Nor could he consider the alleged visions of Jesus reportedly experienced by a boy, Emmanuel Segastasha, from 1982. On July 2, 2001, the Holy See released the bishop's declaration regarding the apparitions.[10]

On November 28, 1992, the first stone was laid for the new shrine, and more than a decade later in 2003, Cardinal Crescenzio Sepe, prefect of the Congregation for the Evangelization of Peoples, consecrated the Shrine of Our Lady of Sorrows, whose construction and name were requested twice by the Virgin in 1982.

The Vision Continues

Bishop Misago, in preparation for the November 28, 2006, feast day celebrations of the twenty-fifth anniversary of the apparitions, promoted the Kibeho message of "striving for reconciliation with enemies; asking forgiveness of people we have offended; respecting others; being tolerant in the family, with neighbors, at work, in meetings and other social events."[11]

The national shrine of Kibeho continues to serve two important purposes. First, it is a memorial for all the lives lost in the 1994 genocide. Second, it is also a crucial reminder to the peoples and nations of the world of the apparitions themselves, when the Virgin Mary appeared as the "Mother of the Word." This gentle, smiling image is a constant reminder that we must continually turn to Christ through Mary in repentance, seeking forgiveness in order that a tragedy on such a massive scale does not happen again.

At the start of a jubilee anniversary year, the Catholic bishops of Rwanda and Burundi led the celebrations that were attended by thousands of priests, men and women religious, and laypeople from Rwanda, Burundi, the Democratic Republic of the Congo, Tanzania, Uganda, and Europe. During the Mass, apostolic nuncio Archbishop Anselmo Guido Pecorari presented a letter from Pope Benedict XVI, announcing that a plenary indulgence had been granted to pilgrims who visited Kibeho during the jubilee year.[12]

In April 2014, Pope Francis met with the Rwandan bishops for their *ad limina* visit, urging them to be agents of reconciliation. Recalling the Marian apparitions at Kibeho, the pope said, "I commend you all to the maternal protection of the Virgin Mary. I sincerely hope that the Shrine of Kibeho might radiate even more the love of Mary for her children, especially the poorest and most injured, and be for the Church in Rwanda, and beyond, a call to turn with confidence to Our Lady of Sorrows, who accompanies each of us on our way that we might receive the gift of reconciliation and peace."

The visions in Kibeho are the most recently occurring Marian apparitions in the world to receive official recognition from the Vatican, and as such sit on the same level as the famed and widely celebrated apparitions of the Virgin Mary at Fatima and Lourdes.

Mary as "Mother of God" in Scripture and throughout Church History

by Dr. Robert Fastiggi

I n the apparitions at Kibeho, the Blessed Mother revealed herself as "Mother of the Word." This is most significant. As Mother of the Word, Mary plays a vital role in the economy of salvation. She is the Mother of God and our mother, who shows great concern for her children. As Vatican II teaches: "By her maternal charity, she cares for the brethren of her Son, who still journey on earth surrounded by dangers and difficulties, until they are led into the happiness of their true home" (*LG*, 62).

What is the scriptural basis for calling Mary "Mother of God"?

Numerous scriptures identify Mary as the mother of Jesus (e.g., Jn 2:1; Mt 1:18, 2:11, 12:46). Since Jesus is God (cf. Jn 1:1), Mary must be recognized as the one who bore God in her womb: *Theotokos*, the Mother of God. ("Mother of God" is *Theotokos* in Greek.)

Calling Mary the Mother of God does not mean that she is mother of the Trinity or of the divine nature of Jesus; rather, it means that the Person of the Word of God was the child she conceived in her womb and to whom she gave birth.

The prophecy of Isaiah 7:14 is applied to Jesus and Mary in Matthew 1:23. Mary is the virgin who gives birth to Emmanuel ("God is with us"). Probably the strongest scriptural support

for Mary as the Mother of God is found in Luke 1:43, where
Elizabeth speaks of Mary as "mother of my Lord." The Greek
word for Lord used here, *Kyrios*, was used as a translation of
the Hebrew word for God's personal name, YHWH (spoken
by Jews as "Adonai" or "Lord"; see *CCC*, 446). The belief in
Mary as the Mother of God is a solemn dogma of the Catholic
Church (*de fide*) proclaimed at the Council of Ephesus in 431.

What were the circumstances leading to this decision at Ephesus?

Nestorianism, the heresy stemming from Nestorius, patriarch
of Constantinople (ca. 381–451), proposed the Incarnation that
was the conjunction of two subjects (that of the Son of God and
that of the man Jesus) and two natures (human and divine).
Nestorius could not understand how God, who is incapable of
suffering, could suffer on the Cross. He therefore understood
the Incarnation as the inhabitation of Jesus by the Divine Word
of God. The Word dwelt in Jesus' body as in a temple.

   The Nestorian heresy was condemned by the Council of
Ephesus in 431. The council also affirmed Mary as the true
Theotokos (birth-giver of God or Mother of God) in these words:

> We do not say, in fact, that the nature of the Word under-
> went a transformation and became flesh or that it was
> changed into a complete man composed of soul and body.
> Rather, we say that the Word, hypostatically uniting to him-
> self the flesh animated by a rational soul, became man in
> an ineffable and incomprehensible manner. . . . For this was
> not an ordinary man who was at first begotten of the holy
> Virgin, and then the Word descended upon him: rather [the
> Word] united flesh to himself from his Mother's womb and
> is said to have undergone begetting in the flesh in order
> to take to himself flesh of his own. . . . For this reason [the
> holy Fathers] have not hesitated to speak of the holy Virgin
> as the Mother of God (*Theotókon*), not certainly because the
> nature of the Word or his divinity had the origin of its being

from the holy Virgin, but because from her was generated his holy body, animated by a rational soul, a body hypostatically united to the Word: and thus it is said that [the Word] was begotten according to the flesh.[13]

Does the Church of the East still disagree with the West on this point?

The Nestorian heresy is associated with the Church of the East from Mesopotamia, Persia, and other areas in Asia. Recent studies, however, show that the Christology of the Church of the East is more complex than the usual understandings of Nestorianism.[14] Moreover, many members of the Church of the East came back into full Catholic communion between the sixteenth and eighteenth centuries to form the Chaldean Catholic Church. Those who remained separated from Rome form the Assyrian Church of the East today.

In 1994, Pope John Paul II and Mar Dinkha IV, the catholicos-patriarch of the Assyrian Church of the East, issued a Common Christological Declaration, which overcame the Nestorian heresy:

Christ . . . is not an "ordinary man" whom God adopted in order to reside in him and inspire him, as in the righteous ones and the prophets. But the same God the Word, begotten of his Father before all worlds without beginning according to his divinity, was born of a mother without a father in the last times according to his humanity. The humanity to which the Blessed Virgin Mary gave birth always was that of the Son of God himself. That is the reason why the Assyrian Church of the East is praying the Virgin Mary as "the Mother of Christ our God and Savior." In the light of this same faith the Catholic tradition addresses the Virgin Mary as "the Mother of God" and also as "the Mother of Christ." We both recognize the legitimacy and rightness of these expressions of the same faith and we both respect the preference of each Church in her liturgical life and piety.[15]

This joint *Christological Declaration* was a remarkable achievement. It serves as a living witness to the importance of true ecumenical dialogue. It is important for Catholics to realize that other Christian churches and ecclesial communities also recognize Mary as the Mother of God, or *Theotokos*. Most prominent among these would be the Eastern Orthodox churches, as Vatican II affirms (see *Lumen Gentium*, 69). The original Protestant Reformers, Martin Luther (1483–1546) and John Calvin (1509–1564), also recognized Mary as the Mother of God, although Calvin discouraged his followers from referring to Mary under this title.[16]

The recognition of Mary as the Mother of God is as important for Christology as it is for Mariology. If Mary is not truly the Mother of the Word Incarnate, then the Word did not really become flesh and dwell among us (cf. Jn 1:14). According to the Creed of Nicaea-Constantinople (ca. 381), the Eternal Word "came down from heaven and by the power of the Holy Spirit was incarnate of the Virgin Mary and was made man."[17] To become incarnate means that Mary truly conceived the Person of the Word of God in her womb and supplied the flesh of the human nature that God, the Word, assumed.

How was this understanding of Mary as Theotokos *transmitted outside the Council of Ephesus?*

There is evidence that this teaching was brought to the people through the liturgical and devotional life of the faithful. One example is the ancient Marian prayer from the third or fourth century known as the *Sub tuum praesidium,* which refers to Mary as Mother of God. The Byzantine Akathist Hymn, which dates from the fifth or sixth century, likewise extols Mary as *Theotokos.*[18] Many Church Fathers, such as St. Athanasius (ca. 296–373), also speak of Mary as *Theotokos,*[19] which literally means "one bearing God to give birth," or the "birth-giver" of God. *Theotokos*, therefore, can also be translated as "Mother of God."

Following the formal affirmation of Mary as *Theotokos* at the Council of Ephesus in 431, subsequent Church councils also affirmed Mary as the Mother of God. The Council of Chalcedon in 451 taught that "the same Son, our Lord Jesus Christ . . . was begotten from the Father before the ages as to the divinity and in the latter days for us and our salvation was born as to his humanity from Mary the Virgin Mother of God."[20] The Second Council of Constantinople in 553 anathematized any person who would say "the glorious holy Mary, ever virgin is not Mother of God in the true sense . . . but does not confess that she is Mother of God in the true and proper sense since God the Word, begotten from the Father before the ages, became incarnate from her in the latter days."[21] The Lateran Synod of 649, held under Pope Martin I, issued this condemnation in its canon 3:

> If anyone does not, following the holy Fathers, confess properly and truly that holy Mary, ever virgin and immaculate, is Mother of God, since she conceived really and truly of the Holy Spirit, without seed, God the Word himself, who, before all ages, was born of God the Father, and that, in the latter age, she gave birth to him without corruption, her virginity remaining equally inviolate after his birth, let him be condemned.[22]

The dogma of Mary as Mother of God sheds light on many other Marian doctrines and devotions. Because she is the Mother of Christ, the Incarnate Word, she is also the Mother of the Church, which is the Mystical Body of her divine Son. In light of her exalted role as the Mother of God, she is our spiritual mother and a most powerful advocate. Because she is the Mother of Christ the King, she is rightfully honored as the Queen of Heaven who intercedes for us from heaven. Because she is the Mother of the Son of God who is "without sin" (Heb

4:15), she herself was preserved from all stain of sin from the moment of her conception. In this way, the Word of God could assume "nature, not guilt" from his mother.[23] As the Mother of God, Mary assumes the role of a Mediatrix who helps to connect the human race to its divine Savior.

◇◇

Prayer to Our Lady of Kibeho

Holy Mary, Our Lady of Sorrows, teach us to understand the value of the Cross in our lives, so that whatever is still lacking to the sufferings of Christ we may fill up in our own bodies for his Mystical Body, which is the Church.

And when our pilgrimage on this earth comes to an end, may we live eternally with you in the kingdom of Heaven.

Bishop Augustin Misago of the Diocese of Gikongoro, Rwanda
March 25, 2006

QUE SOY
ERA
IMMACULADA COUNCEPCIOU

Mary as Immaculate and All-Holy: Our Lady of Lourdes

From the very beginning, and before time began, the eternal Father chose and prepared for his only-begotten Son a Mother in whom the Son of God would become incarnate. . . . So wondrously did God endow her with the abundance of all heavenly gifts poured from the treasury of his divinity that his mother, ever absolutely free of all stain of sin, all fair and perfect, would possess that fullness of holy innocence and sanctity . . . that she would triumph utterly over the ancient serpent. . . . Therefore, we ourselves . . . have confirmed by our authority a proper Office in honor of the Immaculate Conception, and have with exceeding joy extended its use to the universal Church.

POPE PIUS IX, *Ineffabilis Deus*
1854

I am the Immaculate Conception.

MARY to Bernadette Soubirous
1858

49

Few Marian apparitions in history have been recognized more fully by the Catholic Church than the 1858 visions of Mary reported by a fourteen-year-old French girl, Bernadette Soubirous. Pilgrims to this breathtaking Catholic shrine even today will marvel at how much attention and celebration arose out of the supernatural claims of this simple and saintly young visionary.

Although Mary has at times appeared to the powerful and prominent, far more often she appears to simple souls such as Bernadette, those whom history would have otherwise forgotten. It is this purity, this simplicity, this humility of Our Lady that was infused in her from the first moments of her life by the One who created her, which is why she identifies herself for Bernadette as the "Immaculate Conception." In this chapter we will take a closer look both at this title and at the Marian dogma it references, a dogma that had been formally promulgated and solemnly defined just a few years prior to these miraculous events.

Lourdes, France, 1858

Marie-Bernarde (Bernadette) Soubirous was born on January 7, 1844, the first of six children (two of whom died shortly after birth) born to François Soubirous and Louise Casterot from the small town of Lourdes at the foot of the Pyrenees mountains in France.

Plagued with financial difficulties, Bernadette's family was living in a single basement room in the home of her mother's cousin. Lourdes was not a major cultural center or a place of prominence; it had only about four thousand occupants and was largely disconnected from the whole of France, with inhabitants speaking Occitan, a language only used by the local population in the region. It had also been recently hit with disasters in the years preceding the apparition events. A cholera epidemic had taken many lives, with young Bernadette barely escaping its reach. Droughts had damaged the wheat harvest, and its mills, the major source of its livelihood, had been threatened by the Industrial Revolution. France itself was recovering from the Napoleonic Wars (1803–1815), in which the French Empire and its allies battled against various coalitions of nations led by the United Kingdom.

For the impoverished Soubirous family, times were tough. During the winter of 1857, Bernadette's father was unemployed, and the family had no food and no firewood. It is in this dark context that Bernadette went out and encountered the Virgin Mary, who brought the mercy of God that transformed Bernadette and the entire town, lifting them out of physical and spiritual poverty.

Bernadette first encountered Mary on February 11, 1858, while gathering firewood with her sister and a friend near the nearby grotto of Massabielle. She was searching the ground for a dry place to cross a stream near the grotto when the Virgin Mary appeared in a dazzling light: a "small young lady" dressed in a white veil, a blue girdle, and a yellow rose on each foot. Although her sister and friend could not see the vision, Bernadette could see and hear her clearly; it was the first of eighteen visions she would receive over the next several weeks.

Needing to share with someone the details of her mystical experience after her first encounter, Bernadette confided in her sister Marie, who then told their mother all about it. Louise forbade Bernadette to return to the grotto. At first Bernadette humbly obeyed the directive, but three days later she and her sisters finally persuaded their mother to let her go back to the place of the first encounter. Bernadette witnessed the Virgin again, but it caused such a commotion with the other children that her mother thought that they should not return. However, she relented on the eighteenth, when two influential and curious ladies, Madame Milhet and her seamstress, Antoinette Peyret, received permission to go visit the grotto with Bernadette so that they might ascertain the name of the mysterious woman.

On that occasion when the Virgin appeared, she asked Bernadette to come another fifteen times, promising her "happiness not in this world but in the next." Two days later, the Lady taught Bernadette a secret prayer that she treasured in her heart and recited the rest of her life. Although Bernadette was repeatedly teased and questioned about what she had seen, her testimony never wavered:

> She has the appearance of a young girl of sixteen or seventeen. She is dressed in a white robe, girdled at the waist with a blue ribbon, which flows down all along her robe. She wears upon her head a veil that is also white; this veil gives just a glimpse of her hair then falls down at the back below her waist. Her feet are bare but covered by the last folds of her robe except at the point where a yellow rose shines upon each of them. She holds on her right arm a Rosary of white beads with a chain of gold shining like the two roses on her feet.[1]

The Messages of the Visions

On February 23, the Blessed Virgin appeared to Bernadette in a new vision, bestowing on her "three wonderful secrets" that have never been revealed, and on the following day at the next appearance she stressed a single word: "Penitence." Another vision instructed her to "drink the water of the spring, wash in it, and eat the herb that grew there." Obediently, Bernadette began to dig in the ground near the grotto to find the water where she was to bathe. First mud, then a clear-running stream soon emerged, which formed a small pond from which she drank and washed her face, much to the confusion and dismay of the onlookers who began to be convinced that the young visionary was mentally unstable. This skepticism quickly reversed when this very stream became a source of many healings for visitors to the grotto.

The next day, Bernadette was asked to "kiss the ground on behalf of sinners," and the following day, she was asked to tell the priests of Lourdes that they should build a chapel at the grotto. On March 1, Bernadette reported that she had been told that the people should come in procession to the chapel.

The Investigation by the Church

On February 20, 1858, Dr. Pierre-Romaine Dozous, a well-known local physician, evaluated Bernadette and declared that there was no indication of "nervous excitement." On April 7, 1858, he observed her putting her hand through the flame of a candle without feeling pain or getting burned during her ecstasy. Several witnesses testified to her reverence and total absorption while she was at the grotto; despite the fact that she was repeatedly questioned and cross-examined, her testimony never wavered. She was certain that she had seen "Aquero" (her name for the beautiful lady).[2]

As word spread about the visions, the crowds began to swell at the grotto; they continued to grow with each subsequent reported vision. On March 5, twenty thousand people gathered at the apparition site. The parish priest, Abbé Dominique Peyramale, requested that Our Lady give a sign of a rosebush blooming in winter, much like in the account of Our Lady of Guadalupe in Mexico three centuries prior. However, no such sign was granted, and the priest remained dubious of the authenticity of the visions. This reserve—refusing to get swept up in the excitement and seeking proof of a true supernatural event—represents well the Catholic Church's cautious approach in discerning the miraculous.

Although Abbé Peyramale never visited the grotto during any of the apparitions, he informed his bishop, Monsignor Bertrand-Sévère Mascarou Laurence, of what was being reported. And so, when Bernadette returned to the grotto on March 25 (the Solemnity of the Annunciation), and the Virgin identified herself in Bernadette's native language (Occitan), saying, "*Que*

soy era Immaculado Conceptiou ("I am the Immaculate Conception"), Abbé Peyramale was persuaded of the truth of Bernadette's claims. There was no way that the simple, uneducated
fourteen-year-old would have known of this title of Mary's, as
it had been solemnly declared only a few years prior.

And so, together with his bishop, Abbé Peyramale pur-
chased the grotto and the land around it in 1861. Immediately
they worked to improve the accessibility for visitors, and began
construction on the first of the churches, which is now known
as the Crypt. Even today, these grounds are owned and oper-
ated by the Catholic Church, which welcomes the *malades* (sick
pilgrims) and their helpers and holds two processions daily: the
Blessed Sacrament Procession and the Torchlight Procession.

Bernadette received her final invitation to meet the Lady
at the Grotto on July 16, 1858. A diocesan investigative commission, established on July 28, 1858, examined the apparitions
reported by Bernadette for three and a half years, after which
the bishop of the Diocese of Tarbes declared the apparitions to
be authentic.

On July 4, 1866, Bernadette left Lourdes to join the Sisters
of Charity of Nevers and was given the name of Sr. Mary Bernard. She worked there as sacristan and lived in anonymity and
humility, calling herself "a broom which Our Lady used, but
now I have been put back in my corner." She died on April 16,
1879, at age thirty-five, and was buried in St. Gildard Convent
in Nevers, France.

Testing the Waters: The Church's Response
to the Apparitions of Lourdes

In 1876, the Basilica at Lourdes was consecrated. Four years
later, Pope Leo XIII established February 11 as the feast day of
Our Lady of Lourdes for the Diocese of Tarbes. On November
13, 1907, Pope Pius X proclaimed that it be observed throughout the universal Church. Bernadette was beatified by Pope

Pius X in 1925 and later canonized a saint by Pope Pius XI on December 8, 1933, the Solemnity of the Immaculate Conception.

When Bernadette's remains were exhumed in 1919, it was discovered that her body was incorrupt.[3] In 1925, the body of Bernadette was exhumed a second time and was found still to be in a state of near-perfect incorruption. Since then her remains have been viewed by millions of pilgrims who travel to the Nevers shrine, where her body lies in state in a crystal coffin in the convent chapel. Numerous popes have visited Lourdes, including Pope Benedict XVI, who made a pilgrimage in September 2008 for the 150th anniversary of the apparitions.

Lourdes remains one of the most popular places of pilgrimage in the entire world, with as many as six million visitors arriving each year, many of whom come seeking various kinds of healing. The reported healings and other miracles associated with Lourdes continue to be medically and scientifically studied to determine whether there might be a natural explanation for them.

When the existence of the miraculous spring was first reported, the water was tested to see if it contained any healing properties. Local officials had hoped that they would discover that the Lourdes spring was a mineral-rich hot spring, to compete with the hot springs of other French towns. The mayor of Lourdes was disappointed when testing showed that there was nothing special about the measurable levels of minerals found in the waters.

And yet, it was also abundantly clear that this was no ordinary water. In the early days following the apparitions reported by Bernadette, many inhabitants of Lourdes and other visitors who had washed in the waters claimed miraculous healings. In thanksgiving for these favors, people would post their miracles on the walls of the church until the mere preponderance of the claims required that a formal process be established to review such alleged happenings. In 1859, Professor Henri Vergez of the Faculty of Medicine at Montpellier was appointed to examine the cures. Seven cures were recorded before 1862, lending

credibility to the argument for the recognition of the apparitions by Monsignor Bertrand Laurence, bishop of Tarbes, who
approved the visions as authentic on January 18, 1862.

In 1905, Pope Pius X decreed that claims of miraculous
cures at Lourdes should "submit to a proper process" and be
rigorously investigated. At his instigation, the current Lourdes
Medical Bureau (*Bureau des Constatations Médicales*) was formed
and headed by the bishop of Tarbes. Baron Dr. Georges-Fer-
nand Dunot of Saint-Maclou was named the first director. At
the request of Fr. Remi Sempé, the first rector of the sanctuary,
Dunot moved to Lourdes to ensure that pilgrims who believed
they had been cured would be able to file an official report
before leaving so that each case could undergo a rigorous and
collegial medical verification.

Fr. Sempé played an important role in the development
of the shrine, making sure from the beginning that there was
proper application of scientific study to understand and mon-
itor what was going on, so as to control exaggeration and hys-
teria and to be able to trust in the valid cases and the signs of
grace being manifested at Lourdes. Many thousands of cures
have been claimed at the shrine, with more than 7,500 of such
scientifically inexplicable yet verifiable cures being studied by a
rotating panel of doctors from all over the world. Only a select
few have made it through the complete process, passing the
strict standards set out in the Lambertini Criteria.

The Lambertini Criteria

Established by Italian cardinal (and future Pope Benedict XIV)
Prospero Lambertini (1675–1758) in his five-volume work *De
servorum Dei beatificatione et de beatorum canonizatione,* these
criteria are still used by the Medical Commission of the Congregation for the Causes of Saints at the Vatican to examine
intercessory miracles attributed to the subject of a cause for
beatification and canonization.

When an alleged miracle is reported, it must pass certain criteria in order to prove authentic. The criteria are as follows:

- The illness must be serious and not liable to go away by human means.
- The cure must be instantaneous (the illness cannot progressively get better over the course of years).
- The cure must be complete (in cases of blindness, for example, both eyes must regain sight).
- The cure must be lasting (more than ten years for most diseases).
- There can be no other disease or crisis which could have precipitated the cure.
- There can be no medical treatment that relates to the cure. Cases where treatment has failed or has not yet been administered are the cases most likely to be considered by the International Lourdes Medical Commission.

Patients must report their cures to the medical bureau and then follow up with their own physicians back home to obtain the documentation of their previous condition and have it submitted to the doctors in Lourdes. Additionally, patients must fund their own return trips to Lourdes for follow-up testing over the course of years so that their conditions can be monitored.

On those rare occasions where the panel says that a cure is medically inexplicable, the bishop of the Diocese of Tarbes makes the public announcement that a new miracle at Lourdes has been verified.

A Recently Approved Miracle

In 2018, the seventieth inexplicable cure was announced, that of seventy-nine-year-old Sr. Bernadette Moriau, a religious sister of the Franciscaines Oblates du Coeur de Jesus from Bresles in northern France. For nearly fifty years she had been suffering from a condition known as "cauda equina syndrome," causing one foot to become permanently twisted, requiring her to wear a brace and use a wheelchair; by 1987, she had lost the ability to walk. In 2013, she went to the waters of Lourdes, and when she returned home to her convent, she was able to discard her morphine and, leg braces and, just a few days later, went on a five-kilometer walk in celebration of her cure.

These miraculous signs—the apparitions themselves, the incorrupt body of the visionary, and the ongoing faith-filled testimonies of the pilgrims who make their way to the restorative waters of the holy shrine—all point to the significance of this holy encounter between a simple peasant girl and the one who called herself the Immaculate Conception. The God who preserved Mary from the stain of sin in order to prepare her for her unique role as the Mother of Jesus has conquered sin and death and brings through the waters of baptism the healing our souls need to persevere in faith until we reach our journey's end and are fully restored in heaven.

Mary as "Immaculate and All-Holy" in Scripture and throughout Church History
by Dr. Robert Fastiggi

On the Solemnity of the Annunciation, March 25, 1858, the beautiful lady who had been appearing to a fourteen-year-old French girl named Bernadette Soubirous revealed her identity. Speaking in the local dialect, she said, *"Que soy era Immaculado Conceptiou"* ("I am the Immaculate Conception").[4] Bernadette might have heard the title before, but she really did not grasp its meaning. The title, though, had great significance because four years earlier, in 1854, the dogma of the Immaculate Conception had been solemnly proclaimed by Pope Pius IX.[5]

When the Blessed Mother tells Bernadette, "I am the Immaculate Conception," she speaks in a way similar to Jesus when he says, "I am the resurrection and the life" (Jn 11:25). The title "Immaculate Conception" reveals who Mary is in God's plan. As the Immaculate Conception, Mary is the woman who was predestined to be the all-holy and sinless mother of the Word Incarnate.

What is the connection between Mary's Immaculate Conception and her role as Mother of God?

Mary's predestination to be the Mother of God was affirmed by Pope Pius IX in his 1854 bull, *Ineffabilis Deus*, proclaiming the dogma of the Immaculate Conception:

> God Ineffable—whose ways are mercy and truth, whose will is omnipotence itself, and whose wisdom "reaches from end to end mightily, and orders all things sweetly"— having foreseen from all eternity the lamentable wretchedness of the entire human race which would result from the sin of Adam, decreed, by a plan hidden from the centuries, to complete the first work of his goodness by a mystery yet more wondrously sublime through the Incarnation of the Word. This he decreed in order that man who, contrary to the plan of Divine Mercy had been led into sin by the cunning malice of Satan, should not perish; and in order that what had been lost in the first Adam would be gloriously restored in the Second Adam. From the very beginning, and before time began, the eternal Father chose and prepared for his only-begotten Son a Mother in whom the Son of God would become incarnate and from whom, in the blessed fullness of time, he would be born into this world.[6]

The Second Vatican Council also affirmed Mary as the pre-destined Mother of God and likewise linked Mary's predesti-nation to her role as the Mother of God:

> Predestined from eternity by that decree of divine prov-idence which determined the incarnation of the Word to be the Mother of God, the Blessed Virgin was on this earth the virgin Mother of the Redeemer, and above all others and in a singular way the generous associate and humble handmaid of the Lord. (*LG*, 61)

What, though, does Mary's predestination to be the Mother of God have to do with her Immaculate Conception? The answer is found in the human nature she provided to the Word of God who was predestined to become incarnate in her virginal womb. Mary was predestined to be the Immaculate Conception. She was preserved from the stain of original sin because the Eternal Word, in assuming his human nature from her, became like us in all things but sin (cf. Heb 4:15). Thus, the Word of God could only take his human nature from one who was preserved from all sin (original as well as personal). Pope Leo I offers this explanation:

> [Christ] assumed the form of a servant without the defile-ment of sin, enriching the human without diminishing the divine. . . . He is generated, however, by a new birth: because an inviolate virginity, not knowing concupiscence has supplied the matter of the flesh. . . . From the mother of the Lord, nature, not guilt, was assumed (*Assumpta est de matre Domini natura, non culpa*).[7]

What does the Bible say about the Immaculate Conception?

The Catholic dogma of Mary's plenitude of grace from the moment of her conception finds support in the greeting of the angel in Luke 1:28. Mary is spoken of as "full of grace" (*kecharitoméne*), which in Greek means one who has been and continues to be "favored" or "graced" by God (alternate translations could be "completely graced" or "thoroughly graced"). As Fr. Settimo M. Manelli, F.I., observes:

> [*Kecharitoméne*] is a perfect passive participle, translated as *full of grace*, or as *fore-loved, privileged, gratified*. As perfect passive participle, the Greek word means, "to be enriched by grace in a stable, lasting way." In fact, the Greek perfect denotes an action completed in the past whose effects endure. Hence, the angel greets Mary by announcing that she has been enriched by grace in the past and that the effects of this gift remain. Without doubt this is a singular form of address. No one else in the Bible was ever greeted thus. Only Mary has been so addressed, and this in the moment when she was about to accomplish the "fullness of time," to realize the prophecies of old, and when the Word of God stood ready to take of her our human nature.[8]

Mary is "full of grace" because Jesus, in assuming his human nature, becomes like us in all things but without sin (cf. Heb 4:15). It was, therefore, necessary for him to take his human nature from one who is "full of grace" and free from sin (original as well as personal).

Genesis 3:15 also provides support for Mary's Immaculate Conception. The "woman" of Genesis 3:15 is connected with the "woman" at the wedding at Cana and the "woman" standing at the foot of the Cross (see John 2:4 and 19:26) as well as the "woman" in Revelation 12:1, 6. Mary is the "new woman" and the "new Eve" who gives birth to the "new Adam" who brings forth the "new humanity" redeemed by grace.

How do the writings of the Church Fathers support this teaching?

Early patristic support for the Immaculate Conception is found in St. Justin Martyr (ca. 100–165) and St. Irenaeus (ca. 130–202), who identify Mary as "the New Eve." They contrast Mary (the associate of Christ the Redeemer) with Eve (the associate of Adam, who brings death and sin to humanity).

Although these early Church Fathers did not explicitly affirm Mary's Immaculate Conception, the Eve/Mary parallelism led later Church Fathers to affirm Mary as "all-pure" and sinless. Thus, St. Ephrem of Syria (ca. 306–373) writes: "For on you, O Lord, there is no mark; neither is there any stain in your Mother."[9]

With St. Andrew of Crete (ca. 660–740), there is further development. He exclaims: "Your birth was immaculate, O Virgin Immaculate,"[10] and he says, "let us honor [Mary's] holy conception."[11]

St. Andrew does not explicitly affirm Mary's Immaculate Conception, but he does play a role in the development of the doctrine by comparing Mary to the uncontaminated virgin soil possessed of a "pure human nature" that "receives from God the gift of the original creation and reverts to its original purity."[12] In a similar vein, St. Germanus of Constantinople (ca. 635–733) speaks of Mary as "wholly without stain."[13]

It is St. John of Damascus (ca. 690–749), however, who most explicitly affirms the doctrine of Mary's original holiness. In praising the holiness of Mary's conception, he writes:

> Oh blessed loins of Joachim, whence the all-pure seed (*spérma panámomon*) was poured out. Oh glorious womb of Anna, in which the most holy fetus grew and was formed.[14]

Francis Dvornik wrote that this passage provides "a direct proof that John regarded Mary as exempt from all sin from the moment of her passive conception. In other words, the Catholic dogma of the Immaculate Conception is clearly expressed in this statement."[15] Thus, we can see that one of the most eminent Eastern Fathers of the Church affirmed the Catholic dogma of the Immaculate Conception in terms of Mary's original holiness and preservation from all defilement of sin.

What liturgical developments have been associated with this teaching?

Affirmation of the Immaculate Conception also developed liturgically. There was a feast in honor of Mary's conception by St. Anne celebrated in the monasteries of Palestine as early as the seventh century.[16] By the sixth or seventh century, a similar feast developed in the Greek Church, celebrating Mary's conception by St. Anne on December 9.[17] From Greece, the feast spread to Italy and other parts of Western Europe, including Ireland and England.[18]

The question might be asked: Why would there be a feast day celebrating Mary's conception unless there was an intuition that something extraordinary occurred at the time of her conception?

What theological and Magisterial support did the development of this dogma receive?

The theological development of the dogma of the Immaculate Conception can be traced to the Christological developments in the first centuries of the Church, which explored the link between Mary's holiness and the sinless human nature assumed by Christ.

Although Christ, the Incarnate Word, was sent by the Father "in the likeness of sinful flesh and sin" (Rom 8:3), Christ himself was sinless. In its profession of faith, the eleventh Council of Toledo of 675 proclaimed:

> We believe, according to the truth of the Gospel, that in the form of man that was assumed, He, who "was made sin" [cf. 2 Cor 5:21] for our sake alone, that is, as the sacrifice for our sins, was conceived without sin, born without sin [and] died without sin.[19]

The assumption of the guilt of sin by Christ was, therefore, vicarious. He assumed "the likeness of sin" in order to redeem sinful humanity. The sinless Word of God, it was reasoned, would need to take his human nature from a human mother who herself was without sin. The question, though, was whether Mary was *purified* of original sin or *preserved* from it at the moment of her conception.

Many Latin theologians of the Middle Ages (e.g., St. Bernard of Clairvaux, St. Albert the Great, and St. Thomas Aquinas) believed Mary needed to be purified from original sin because Christ is the universal Redeemer. Although St. Thomas Aquinas believed that after Christ, "the purity of the Blessed Virgin holds the highest place,"[20] he nevertheless held that "if the soul of the Blessed Virgin had never incurred the stain of original sin, it would be derogatory to the dignity of Christ, by reason of His being the universal Savior of all."[21] Therefore, he concluded that "the Blessed Virgin did indeed contract original sin, but was cleansed therefrom before her birth from the womb."[22] St. Thomas, therefore, believed Mary was born free from original sin, but she was not conceived free from original sin.

Later theologians such as William of Ware (ca. 1255–1305) and Bl. John Duns Scotus (ca. 1266–1308) recognized the logic of St. Thomas's position, but they proposed that the merits of Christ, the Redeemer, could be applied to Mary by means of "anticipatory redemption" or "pre-redemption" (*praeredemptio*) in anticipation of her future role as the Mother of the Word Incarnate.[23]

The position of Scotus provided a means of joining Christ's redemptive work to Mary's preservation from original sin. As Fr. Peter Fehlner, F.I., explains, the position of Scotus in no way detracts from the merit of Christ on the Cross. Indeed, "a preservative rather than liberative redemption of Mary . . . enhances the greatness of the redemptive work *qua* redemptive."[24] By replacing "purification or liberation from sin" with "preservation from sin," Scotus "revolutionized the entire discussion and opened the road to a dogmatic definition."[25]

The theological solution offered by Scotus led to debates about the subject between the Franciscans and the Dominicans.

Pope Sixtus IV, a Franciscan, did much to move the faithful toward a fuller acceptance of Mary's special privilege of grace. In 1477, he approved a feast day in honor of Mary's Immaculate Conception, and in 1483, he censured those who attacked this feast.[26] In its decree on original sin in 1546, the Council of Trent stopped short of a full definition of Mary's Immaculate Conception. However, the bishops at Trent made it clear that it was not their intention to include in this decree "the blessed and immaculate Virgin Mary, the Mother of God."[27]

After Trent, the Catholic Magisterium continued to move toward a complete affirmation of Mary's Immaculate Conception. In 1567, Pope Pius V, in his list of the errors of Michel de Bay, included the opinion that Mary died because of the sin contracted from Adam.[28] In 1617, Pope Paul V forbade any public attacks against the doctrine of Mary's preservation from original sin.[29] In 1661, Pope Alexander VII published his brief, *Sollicitudo omnium ecclesiarum*, manifesting his support for the Immaculate Conception. Although he did not make belief in the Immaculate Conception mandatory, he affirmed his favor toward the feast and doctrine in these words:

> We, considering that the holy Roman Church solemnly celebrates the feast of the conception of the spotless and ever-virgin Mary and for a long while has established for this a special and proper Office . . . and wishing to promote . . . this praiseworthy piety and devotion and the feast and the cult . . . we renew . . . [the decrees] promulgated on behalf of the judgment which affirms that the soul of the blessed Virgin Mary in its creation and its infusion into the body was blessed by the grace of the Holy Spirit and preserved from original sin.[30]

Following this special papal endorsement of Mary's Immaculate Conception, those who denied Mary's privilege were seen more and more as opponents of a Catholic doctrine. In 1690, the Holy Office published a decree condemning thirty

Jansenist theses, including the view that Mary needed purification from sin.[31]

Pope Clement XI, in his constitution *Commissi nobis divinitus* of December 6, 1708, extended the Solemnity of the Immaculate Conception of Mary to the entire Catholic Church. The apparition of Mary to St. Catherine Labouré in Paris in 1830 provided devotional support for the doctrine. The special "miraculous medal" associated with the apparition contained the prayer: "O Mary conceived without sin, pray for us who have recourse to thee."[32]

By the mid-nineteenth century, Catholic support for the Immaculate Conception was widespread. The US bishops, at the sixth provincial council of Baltimore in 1846, decided to petition the pope for permission to have Mary, under the title of the Immaculate Conception, be the patroness of the Catholic Church in the United States; Pope Pius IX acceded to this request in 1847.

In his encyclical *Ubi primum* of 1849, Pope Pius IX asked his brother bishops whether they wished the Holy See to define the Immaculate Conception as a dogma. Of the 603 bishops who were consulted, 546 responded in favor of the definition and only four or five stated that they did not believe the doctrine could be defined. Moved by the clear manifestation of collegial support from the Catholic episcopacy, Pope Pius IX, on December 8, 1854, issued the following definition:

> To the honor of the holy and undivided Trinity, to the glory and distinction of the Virgin Mother of God, for the exaltation of the Catholic faith and the increase of the Christian religion, by the authority of our Lord, Jesus Christ, of the blessed apostles Peter and Paul and our own authority, we declare, pronounce and define: the doctrine, which maintains that the most blessed Virgin Mary, at the first instant of her conception, by the singular grace and privilege of almighty God and in view of the merits of Jesus Christ, the

Savior of the human race, was preserved immune from all stain of original sin, is revealed by God and, therefore, firmly and constantly to be believed by all the faithful.[33]

How are the apparitions at Lourdes significant in this regard?

The apparitions of the Blessed Mother to St. Bernadette in 1858 gave Mary's personal support for the dogma infallibly proclaimed by the Roman pontiff. Mary's Immaculate Conception enables her to be fully devoted to the work of her divine Son without any impediment of sin, as we read in *Lumen Gentium:*

> Adorned from the first instant of her conception with the radiance of an entirely unique holiness, the Virgin of Nazareth is greeted, on God's command, by an angel messenger as "full of grace" (Lk 1:28) and to the heavenly messenger she replies: "Behold the handmaid of the Lord, be it done unto me according to thy word" (Lk 1:38). Thus Mary, a daughter of Adam, consenting to the divine Word, became the mother of Jesus, the one and only Mediator. Embracing God's salvific will with a full heart and impeded by no sin, she devoted herself totally as a handmaid of the Lord to the person and work of her Son, under Him and with Him, by the grace of almighty God, serving the mystery of redemption. *(LG, 56)*

The mystery of redemption includes God's love for the poor, the sick, and the suffering. Our Lady of Lourdes is the Immaculate Mother who manifests her compassion toward those in pain. Pope Pius XII, in his 1957 encyclical, *Le Pelèrinage de Lourdes*, spoke eloquently of the Immaculate Virgin Mary's compassion for those who suffer:

> And if in her solicitude Mary looks upon some of her children with a special predilection, is it not, Beloved Sons and Venerable Brothers, upon the lowly, the poor, and the afflicted whom Jesus loved so much? "Come to me, all you

who labor and are burdened, and I will give you rest," she seems to say along with her divine Son.

Go to her, you who are crushed by material misery, defenseless against the hardships of life and the indifference of men. Go to her, you who are assailed by sorrows and moral trials. Go to her, beloved invalids and infirm, you who are sincerely welcomed and honored at Lourdes as the suffering members of our Lord. Go to her and receive peace of heart, strength for your daily duties, joy for the sacrifice you offer. (*Le Pèlerinage de Lourdes*, 56–57)

◇◇

PRAYER TO OUR LADY OF LOURDES ⚜

Mary, you who appeared to Bernadette in the hollow of the rock, in the cold and depths of winter, you brought the warmth of a presence, the friendship of a smile, the light and beauty of grace.

In the hollow of our often-obscure lives, in the hollow of this world where evil is powerful, bring hope, restore confidence.

You who said to Bernadette, "I am the Immaculate Conception": come to the help of the sinners that we are. Give us the courage of conversion, the humility of penance, and the perseverance of prayer.

We entrust to you all those we carry in our hearts and especially the sick and those in despair, you who are "Our Lady of Good Help." You guided Bernadette to the spring. Guide us to him who is the source of eternal life, the One who gave us the Holy Spirit, so that we dare to say: *Our Father who art in Heaven. . . .* Amen.[34]

Mary as Mother of Sorrows: Our Lady of La Salette

> If, when you say to the people what I have said to you so far, and what I will still ask you to say, if, after that, they do not convert, (if they do not do penance, and they do not cease working on Sunday, and if they continue to blaspheme the Holy Name of God), in a word, if the face of the earth does not change, God will be avenged.
>
> OUR LADY OF LA SALETTE to Mélanie Calvat[1]

Many times around the world and throughout Christian history, claims have emerged of miraculous weeping icons and statues, with myrrh, human tears, or blood streaming forth from a statue of the Virgin Mary. These instances of lacrimation, or the production of tears, demonstrate to us the sorrows of the Mother of God as she contemplates the suffering heart of her Son, pierced anew by the sins of humanity.

In a few rare instances, the Virgin Mary has revealed herself in a very personal way as the Mother of Sorrows, which she did as Our Lady of La Salette in France. In this dramatic appearance, she laid out dire warnings and predicted the onset of tragedies that would befall Europe in general, and France in particular. Following on the heels of the French Revolution and the widespread secularization of France, in 1846 she appeared to eleven-year-old Maximin Giraud and fourteen-year-old Françoise Mélanie Calvat-Mathieu while they tended cows. Her tearful presence six thousand feet up in the French Alps called out to all humanity for the conversion of hearts and penance for sins.

La Salette-Fallavaux, France, 1846

On September 19, 1846, the day after the moveable feast of the Holy Cross and on the day of Our Lady of Sorrows, a glowing globe of light attracted Mélanie and Maximin, who were out tending cows. Both children were from very poor families and had been hired by wealthier families to watch their livestock.

Fascinated and a little fearful, they crept closer for a better look. Inside the glowing light, a beautiful woman sat on a rock, her head in her hands. When she looked up, they saw she was weeping crystal-like tears. The children, from unchurched Catholic families, thought at first that she was a beaten woman or someone running away from harm. When she stood up and beckoned to them, they did not know who she was.

"Come to me, my children," she said. "Do not be afraid. I am here to tell you something of the greatest importance."[2]

She told them how the offenses of men—their refusal to pray and to observe the Sabbath rest—would result in disasters such as famine and disease. She gave each of the children a secret, just as she had to the visionaries at Fatima and Lourdes, and told them to pray. However, unlike these other appearances, Our Lady of La Salette appeared to them only once.

Distinctive Elements of This Apparition and Its Secrets

The fact that Our Lady appeared only once is a bit unusual. At Fatima and at Lourdes, at Kibeho and at Saint-Étienne-le-Laus (France), she is reported to have appeared many times, each time bestowing some part of her message. In other cases, such as in Knock, in Pontmain (France), and here at La Salette, she appeared just on the singular occasion. For different people and different places, the Mother of God appears in what way the visionary, the location, and the time in history need her the most.

In her words given that day at La Salette and meant for the world, the Virgin urged the children, speaking first in formal French and then in *patois*, to renounce sin and turn to God in penance. A failure to do so, she said, would bring on great punishment at the hands of Divine Justice: "If my people will not obey, I shall be compelled to loose my Son's arm. It is so heavy, so pressing that I can no longer restrain it. How long I have suffered for you!"[3]

Rising from her seated position, the beautiful woman crossed her arms over her chest and expressed deep sorrow at her suffering due to the sins of humanity against her Son, and the need for her constant intercession on behalf of humanity to forestall the punishment that was justly due to men. The Virgin also lamented the common practice of disrespecting her Son's holy name and related it to the ongoing potato famine that had begun the previous year and which was meant to serve as a sign: "I warned you last year by means of the potatoes. You paid no heed. Quite the reverse, when you discovered that the potatoes had rotted, you swore, you abused my Son's name. They will continue to rot and by Christmas this year there will be none left."[4]

Likewise she shed light on the general loss of belief among the people and the diminishment of authentic religious practice: "Only a few rather old women go to Mass in the summer. All the rest of the people work every Sunday throughout the summer. And in winter, when they don't know what to do with themselves, they go to Mass only to poke fun at religion. During Lent they flock to the butcher shops, like dogs. . . . My children . . . you will make this known to all people."[5]

She foretold of an upcoming famine in the region and the resulting tragedies that would ensue: "If you have grain, it will do you no good to sow it, for what you sow the beasts will devour, and any part of it that springs up will crumble into dust when you thresh it. A great famine is coming. But before that happens, the children under seven years of age will be seized with trembling and die in their parents' arms. The grownups will pay for their sins by hunger. The grapes will rot, and the walnuts will turn bad."[6]

Despite the sorrows that would befall France, the Virgin reaffirmed her hope in humanity and urged the conversion of hearts that could quickly reverse the punishments: "If people are converted, the rocks will become piles of wheat, and it will be found that the potatoes have sown themselves."[7] The children were each given a secret that they later recorded for Church authorities. The woman again vanished in a glowing globe of light, and the children began to talk to the people about what they had seen and heard.

Sadly, her message went largely unheeded, and in December 1846, as she foretold, many crops—including potatoes, grapes, and walnuts—were decimated with disease. The following year, a famine throughout Europe resulted in approximately one million deaths, including one hundred thousand in France alone. An epidemic of cholera swept through France and took the lives of many children, as projected in Our Lady's dire warnings.

The Church's Response

News of the apparition spread quickly. In September 1846, Msgr. Philibert de Bruillard of Grenoble, the bishop of the diocese, began an official inquiry into the alleged supernatural events. During the investigation conducted by the local authorities, the children were taken to the site of the apparition. A man broke off a piece of rock at the spot of the Virgin's appearance and uncovered a healing spring that resulted in twenty-three verified cures within the first year. By October 1846, the prophecies of La Salette had become widely circulated.

In August 1848, the bishop appointed one of the best theologians in the diocese, his vicar general, Fr. Pierre Joseph Rousselot, as official investigator into the apparitions. Rousselot addressed twelve objections to the reality of the purported apparition events in his report titled *La vérité sur l'événement de La Salette* ("The Truth about the Event of La Salette"), which was sent to Pope Pius IX.

Of all the reported details related to this singular apparition, none ignited more controversy than the so-called Secret of La Salette, which predicted great turmoil for the Church and calamities for the earth. On July 3, 1851, Maximin and Mélanie wrote it down for the bishop in the presence of Church officials. Three days later, Mélanie rewrote the secret in order to fix a chronological error she had noticed. The letters were then taken by messenger to Pope Pius IX.[8]

On September 19, 1851, Msgr. de Bruillard released a pastoral letter for the fifth anniversary of the La Salette apparition, declaring that it was worthy of belief by the faithful in the supernatural character of the event, saying that it "bears in itself all the characteristics of the truth, and that the faithful are justified in believing without question in its truth."[9]

In further signs of episcopal approval, the following May Msgr. de Bruillard initiated the construction of a shrine near the location of the apparition at the center of a mountain ring formed by the Gargas and the Chamoux. He also established the order of the Missionaries of Our Lady of La Salette to staff the shrine, which was completed and consecrated in 1879. France's First National Pilgrimage to La Salette occurred on August 18, 1872; seven hundred pilgrims arrived from Paris and were later joined by other groups from Dijon, Ars, and Lyons.

The Seers' Final Years

Although the messages of Our Lady of La Salette received the approval of the local bishop, the children to whom her secrets had been entrusted continued to struggle in their lives.

Maximin joined the seminary after the apparitions, but he did not become a priest. The remainder of his years were spent in travel and various short-term jobs. He died on March 1, 1875, affirming the truth of the La Salette apparitions until the end.

Mélanie entered religious life and transferred orders several times over the years. Her rewriting and expanding of the La Salette secret in 1879 created controversy and ignited ongoing disputes that continue to the present. After a lifetime of being in and out of the public eye, Mélanie moved to Altamura, Italy, where she lived in anonymity and died December 15, 1904.

The complicated stories of these two visionaries underscore that God does not always choose perfect or saintly messengers, even in these cases of authentic apparitions. While one might expect that a visitation from the Mother of God might induce one to lead an exemplary life, we are all given free will.

Therefore, let us remember how these two welcomed the Virgin Mary and related both the events and her messages. La Salette should not be forgotten: the tears from the heart of a mother remind us to turn back to her Son and begin with our own conversion.

Mary as "Mother of Sorrows" in Scripture and throughout Church History

by Dr. Robert Fastiggi

O ur Lady of La Salette reminds us that Mary is the Mother of Sorrows. On Tuesdays and Fridays, Catholics pray the Sorrowful Mysteries of the Rosary, which recall the events of Christ's Passion, beginning with his agony in the garden and culminating with his death on the Cross. The inseparable bond between Jesus and Mary unites them in suffering as well as in joy and glory.[10]

Is Mary depicted as Our Lady of Sorrows in scripture?

At the presentation in the Temple, Simeon tells Mary that a sword shall pierce her own heart or soul (see Luke 2:35). The piercing of Mary's heart took place at Calvary, where she underwent her own passion in union with her divine Son dying on the Cross. Pope John Paul II, in his 1984 apostolic letter, *Salvifici Doloris*, offered this moving summary of Mary's communion in the suffering of her divine Son:

> [It] was on Calvary that Mary's suffering, beside the suffering of Jesus, reached an intensity which can hardly be imagined from a human point of view but which was mysterious and supernaturally fruitful for the redemption of the world. Her ascent of Calvary and her standing at the foot of the Cross together with the Beloved Disciple were a special sort of sharing in the redeeming death of her Son. And the words which she heard from his lips were a kind

of solemn handing-over of this Gospel of suffering so that it
could be proclaimed to the whole community of believers.

As a witness to her Son's Passion by her *presence,* and
as a sharer in it by her *compassion,* Mary offered a unique
contribution to the "Gospel of suffering," by embodying in
anticipation the expression of St. Paul which was quoted
at the beginning. She truly has a special title to be able to
claim that she "completes in her flesh"—as already in her
heart—"what is lacking in Christ's afflictions." (*Salvifici
Doloris,* 25)

The sorrows of Mary have been a frequent subject of Catholic art and devotion. We only need to recall the famous *Pietà*
of Michelangelo or the medieval hymn *Stabat Mater,* attributed
to Jacopone da Todi (1230–1306). This hymn draws near to
the crucified Christ in communion with his suffering mother.
Devotion to the Sorrows of Mary grew in the Middle Ages, and
the Servite Order, founded in 1233, promoted devotion to the
seven sorrows of Mary.

What are the seven sorrows of Mary?

The seven sorrows are mostly found in scripture, and can be
summarized as follows:

1. the prophecy of Simeon (Lk 2:25–35);
2. the flight into Egypt (Mt 2:13–15);
3. the loss of the child Jesus in the Temple (Lk 2:43–45);
4. Mary's meeting of Jesus on the way of the Cross;
5. Mary under the Cross at Calvary (Jn 19:25);
6. the piercing of the side of Jesus with a sword and his
   descent from the Cross (Jn 19:31–38); and
7. the burial of Jesus (Jn 19:40–42).

What Marian feast days are associated with this devotion?

The feast of Our Lady of Sorrows, promoted by the Servite Order since the fifteenth century as the feast of the Seven Dolors (or Sorrows) of Mary, is now celebrated on September 15. Local celebrations of this feast go back to the twelfth century. In 1814, Pope Pius VII declared it to be a universal feast.

Devotion to the Seven Dolors of Mary is often linked to her sorrowful Immaculate Heart.

What is the origin of the devotion to Mary's heart?

Devotion to Mary's heart became prominent in the Middle Ages. Simeon Metaphrastes (ca. 900–984), depicts Mary addressing her beloved Son and saying: "Your side has been pierced, but my heart has been pierced also."[11]

Arnold of Chartres (Bonneval) (died ca. 1158) said that Jesus and Mary "offered but one holocaust to God; Mary by the blood of her heart; Christ by the blood of his body."[12]

Among those who promoted devotion to Mary's heart are Eckbert of Schönau (d. 1184); St. Mechtild of Hackeborn (1240–1298); St. Gertrude the Great (1256–1302); and St. Bridget of Sweden (1303–1373). The Blessed Mother appeared to St. Bridget and told her how she participated in her Son's suffering under the Cross "because his heart was my heart."[13] The Blessed Mother went on to say: "Just as Adam and Eve sold the world for one apple, so my Son and I redeemed the world, as it were, with one heart."[14]

In the seventeenth century, devotion to Mary's heart was found in St. Francis de Sales (1567–1622) and most especially in St. John Eudes (1601–1680), who taught the mystical union of the Hearts of Jesus and Mary. St. Margaret Mary Alacoque (1647–1690) also reported having a vision of three hearts: two were very luminous and bright with one being much brighter than the other; the third heart was very small. She came to understand that the two brighter hearts were those of Jesus and Mary and the third heart was her own.

St. Louis de Montfort (1673–1716) noted that the heart of Mary was pierced through at the side of Christ on the Cross.[15] The Jesuit Pierre-Joseph Clorivière (1735–1820) helped to establish the Priests of the Heart of Jesus and the Daughters of the Heart of Mary.[16]

The sorrows of Mary are prominent in the apparitions of La Salette (1846) and Fatima (1917). In 1916, the year before the Fatima apparitions, the Angel of Peace (or Angel of Portugal) gave Holy Communion to the three shepherd children, teaching them this prayer:

> O Most Holy Trinity, Father, Son, and Holy Spirit, I adore Thee profoundly. I offer Thee the most precious Body, Blood, Soul, and Divinity of Jesus Christ, present in all the tabernacles of the world, in reparation for the outrages, sacrileges, and indifference by which He is offended. By the infinite merits of the Sacred Heart of Jesus and the Immaculate Heart of Mary, I beg the conversion of poor sinners.

Why is devotion to the Immaculate Heart of Mary important?

The apparition at La Salette reveals the sorrows of the Blessed Mother. These sorrows pertain to the heart of Mary. At Fatima on June 13, 1917, the Lady revealed to Lucia Santos that God wished to establish in the world devotion to her Immaculate Heart and her heart would be a refuge and a way to lead people to God.

On December 10, 1925, when Lucia was a religious sister living in Pontevedra, Spain, Mary appeared to her with the Child Jesus; she requested the devotion of the five first Saturdays in reparation to her Immaculate Heart. On June 13, 1929, when Sister Lucia was in Tuy, Spain, the Blessed Mother gave Sister Lucia a vision of the Most Holy Trinity and said that the time had come for the consecration of Russia to her Immaculate

Heart. This consecration was carried out on March 25, 1984, by Pope John Paul II in St. Peter's Square.

In his May 15, 1956, encyclical *Haurietis aquas*, ("On Devotion to the Sacred Heart"), Pope Pius XII spoke of the intrinsic connection between the hearts of Jesus and Mary, why it is only right to offer devotion to them both:

> For, by God's Will, in carrying out the work of human Redemption the Blessed Virgin Mary was inseparably linked with Christ in such a manner that our salvation sprang from the love and the sufferings of Jesus Christ to which the love and sorrows of His Mother were intimately united. It is, then, entirely fitting that the Christian people— who received the divine life from Christ through Mary— after they have paid their debt of honor to the Sacred Heart of Jesus should also offer to the most loving Heart of their heavenly Mother the corresponding acts of piety affection, gratitude and expiation. (*Haurietis aquas*, 124)

What is the triumph of the Immaculate Heart of Mary predicted by Mary at Fatima?

On June 26, 2000, Cardinal Ratzinger offered this reflection:

> The Heart open to God, purified by contemplation of God, is stronger than guns and weapons of every kind. The *fiat* of Mary, the word of her heart, has changed the history of the world, because it brought the Savior into the world— because, thanks to her *Yes*, God could become man in our world and remains so for all time. The Evil One has power in this world, as we see and experience continually; he has power because our freedom continually lets itself be led away from God. But since God himself took a human heart and has thus steered human freedom toward what is good, the freedom to choose evil no longer has the last word.

From that time forth, the word that prevails is this: "In the world you will have tribulation, but take heart; I have overcome the world" (Jn 16:33).

What is the connection between the Immaculate Heart and Our Lady of Sorrows?

Because Mary's heart was never touched by sin—original or personal—it is intimately united to the Sacred Heart of her divine Son. On Calvary, our Lord poured out his heart in love for the sins of mankind. Our Blessed Mother, the Mother of Sorrows, stood under the Cross and united her heart to the heart of her Son in suffering and in love. Pope Pius X's successor, Benedict XV, in his 1918 letter *Inter Sodalicia* wrote that Mary renounced her maternal rights and, "as far as it depended on her, offered her Son to placate divine justice; so we may well say that she, with Christ, redeemed mankind."[17]

Mary, as Our Lady of Sorrows, continues to show her maternal love to all the children of her Son. As a good mother she shares also in the suffering and trials of her spiritual children on earth. As Mother of Sorrows, she knows what it is to suffer. Therefore, she can emphathize with all those who suffer here in this "valley of tears." Mary, as our Immaculate and Sorrowful Mother, not only cares for us in physical pain, but she also cares for us spiritually. As Vatican II teaches:

> This maternity of Mary in the order of grace began with the consent which she gave in faith at the Annunciation and which she sustained without wavering beneath the cross, and lasts until the eternal fulfillment of all the elect. Taken up to heaven she did not lay aside this salvific duty, but by her constant intercession continued to bring us the gifts of eternal salvation. By her maternal charity, she cares for the brethren of her Son, who still journey on earth surrounded by dangers and difficulties, until they are led into the happiness of their true home. (*LG*, 62)

◇◇

PRAYER TO OUR LADY OF LA SALETTE ⚜

D ear Lady of La Salette, true Mother of Sorrows, Remember the tears that you shed for me at Calvary; and the unceasing care with which you shield me from the justice of God. I beg you, do not abandon your child, for whom you have done so much. Inspired by this consoling thought, I cast myself at your feet, despite my infidelity and ingratitude.

Reject not my prayer, O Virgin of reconciliation. Obtain for me the grace to love Jesus Christ above all things, and to console your heart by living a holy life, that one day I may be able to see you in heaven. Amen.

Chapter 6

Mary as Mediatrix of Grace: Our Lady of the Miraculous Medal

> My child, the good God wishes to charge you with a mission. You will have much to suffer, but you will rise above these sufferings by reflecting that what you do is for the glory of God.
>
> First Apparition of Our Lady of Rue du Bac
> to Catherine Labouré
> July 18, 1830

> Have a Medal struck after this model. All who wear it will receive great graces; they should wear it around the neck. Graces will abound for persons who wear it with confidence.
>
> Second Apparition of Our Lady of Rue du Bac
> to Catherine Labouré
> November 27, 1830

Catholics around the world seek the assistance of the Virgin Mary as their greatest intercessor with her Son, who scripture tells us is the "one mediator between God and the human race" (1 Tm 2:5). Mary's intercessory role, then, is inextricably linked to that of her Son (see *CCC*, 964) as well as her role as "mother . . . in the order of grace" (*CCC*, 968).

"Therefore the Blessed Virgin is invoked in the Church under the titles of Advocate, Helper, Benefactress, and Mediatrix" (*CCC*, 969).

The efficacy of Mary's role as Mediatrix of Grace can be clearly seen in the many Marian miracles, favors, and blessings attested to throughout history by saints and sinners alike. Along with the Rosary, the Miraculous Medal is among the most popular of Marian sacramentals, connecting the Blessed Mother with the faithful all over the world. Reproduced more than a billion times, the design for the ubiquitous medal was received in supernatural fashion through apparitions to St. Catherine Labouré, who was then a novice in the French order of religious sisters known as the Daughters of Charity.

Paris, France, 1830

The daughter of a yeoman farmer, Catherine Labouré, known as Zoe to her family, was born on May 2, 1806, the ninth of eleven children, at Fain-les-Moûtiers (near Dijon), Côte d'Or, France. After her mother died when Catherine was just nine years old, the little girl became close to the Mother of God, whom she came to regard as her own mother. Catherine remembered her mother's advice to "run to Mary," and she drew strength from that advice after her mother's death.

After Catherine received her first Holy Communion at the age of twelve, she had a deep desire to pursue a vocation in religious life like her elder sister Louisa, who had joined the Sisters of Charity. Her father was not in favor of this, and in 1824, he sent her to attend finishing school in Paris. However, Catherine was determined to answer the call to religious life, and so she rejected her father's recommended suitors, telling him that she was promised to Christ.

In January 1830, Catherine's father relented and gave her permission to enter the Daughters of Charity. Catherine went to work at the Hospice de la Charité in Châtillon-sur-Seine. Her postulancy lasted three months, after which she went to live at the motherhouse of the Daughters of Charity of St. Vincent de Paul at 140 Rue du Bac in Paris.

The Visions Begin

On April 30 of that year, Catherine told her confessor that she had experienced a vision of what she believed to be the heart of St. Vincent de Paul, the patron of her order. In the months that followed, she also saw Christ appear to her at Communion and during adoration. At the time, her confessor dismissed the experiences as being the product of her imagination. Nevertheless, Catherine asked St. Vincent to pray for her, that God would grant her the special favor of seeing the Virgin Mary.

On July 18, 1830, her prayers were answered. Late that night Catherine was awakened and led by a "shining child" to the empty chapel, which was illuminated by candles as if it were midnight Mass. There, a noise "like the rustling of a silk dress" moved toward her and she looked up to see the Virgin Mary. Catherine scrambled to kneel on the altar steps and rest her hands on the knees of her heavenly visitor in what she would call the "happiest moment in my life."[1]

The Virgin Mary talked with her for hours, telling her that she would have to undertake a difficult task and warning her of a great time of upheaval that would occur in France and beyond: "My child, the good God wishes to charge you with a mission. . . . You will have much to suffer. But do not be afraid."[2]

Later, Catherine requested an explanation. The Virgin told her that the world would be hit by calamities and that France specifically would be overwhelmed with difficulty and "the throne will be destroyed." She also offered Catherine great hope and reminded her that she was the Mediatrix of Grace, pouring out graces on all who ask, "great or small." She assured Catherine of her watchful protection and that she would grant her many graces. "Especially will graces be shed upon those who ask for them."[3]

When in July of that year Catherine told her spiritual director of these visions, Fr. Jean Marie Aladel told Catherine that her experience had been only a dream or from her imagination and that she should try to ignore these thoughts.

The Miraculous Medal

On November 27, 1830, Mary appeared to Catherine a second time in the same chapel. This time she appeared while Catherine was praying with her sisters who did not see the vision. As Catherine watched the moving figure, an oval encircled the Blessed Mother with the words *Ô Marie, conçue sans péché, priez pour nous qui avons recours à vous* ("O Mary, conceived without sin, pray for us who have recourse to thee").[4]

A voice instructed Catherine to have a medal struck after the image she was seeing: Mary standing on a globe, with light streaming from the jewels on the rings on her fingers, symbolizing her distribution of graces to all those around the world who ask for them. Some of the jewels on the Virgin's rings were not emanating graces in shafts of light, indicating "the graces for which souls forget to ask."[5]

On the reverse side of the picture appeared a capital M with a cross and two hearts: one above for Jesus, crowned with thorns, and one for Mary, pierced with a sword. The voice promised that all who wore this sacramental would receive great graces: "Those who wear it blessed about their necks, and who confidently say this prayer will receive great graces and will enjoy the special protection of the Mother of God."[6]

The Medal Is Struck

Catherine went again to Fr. Aladel, who again attributed what she had seen to "too much imagination." He did nothing more until September 1831, when the Blessed Mother appeared a final time and reproached Catherine for not making progress on the medal. Catherine again sincerely approached her confessor, Fr. Aladel, and this time he believed her, having observed

Catherine's normal daily behavior for nearly two years. He then approached Archbishop de Quélen of Paris with the Virgin's request and obtained permission for a medal to be struck.

Within a month, the first fifteen hundred Miraculous Medals were struck, and by the end of 1833, fifty thousand medals had been given out. The popularity of the medal grew, especially after the conversion of Alphonse Ratisbonne in 1842. Alphonse was an Alsatian Jew who, having been persuaded to wear the medal as a test, received a vision of Mary in the church of Sant'Andrea delle Fratte at Rome, converted instantaneously, became a priest, and founded the religious congregation known as the Sisterhood of Our Lady of Sion.

Catherine was then sent to the Enghien-Reuilly convent outside of Paris as prioress, where she would devote the remaining forty years of her life to the care of the elderly in the Hospice d'Enghien. Although Catherine experienced only those few visible apparitions, she continued to experience locutions, interior voices of Mary. However, she spoke of this to no one other than her confessor, and when Fr. Aladel died in 1865, no one alive had heard her full story of the visions.

On July 13, 1836, the archbishop began an official canonical inquiry into the apparitions. Based on the reliability of her confessor and the reputation of Catherine's character, the tribunal validated the authenticity of the visions. In his official statement of approval, Archbishop of Paris Hyacinthe-Louis de Quélen wrote,

> . . . [T]he prodigious number of medals that have been stamped and distributed, the stunning benefits and singular graces . . . truly seem to be the signs by which heaven has wished to confirm the reality of the apparitions, the truth of the report of the visionary and the diffusion of the medal.[7]

Toward the end of Catherine's life, she received permission from the Virgin Mary to share her story, so she revealed her identity as the visionary of the Miraculous Medal to her superior, Sr. Dufé. On December 31, 1876, Catherine died. Her incorrupt body remains in the convent chapel at the Rue du Bac and is to this day seen by many visiting pilgrims. "And thus when she came to the end of her mortal life," wrote Fr. Joseph Dirwin in his biography of St. Catherine, "she did not face death with fear but with gladness. Confident in God and the most holy Virgin, she took time to distribute, with a weak and tremulous hand, the last of her Miraculous Medals to those standing by. Then, content and smiling, she hastened away to heaven."[8]

On July 19, 1931, it was decreed that Catherine had lived a life of heroic virtue and was named venerable by Pope Pius XI. On May 28, 1933, she was beatified by Pope Pius XI, and canonized on July 27, 1947, by Pope Pius XII.

Mary as "Mediatrix of Grace" in Scripture and throughout Church History

by Dr. Robert Fastiggi

The apparition to St. Catherine Labouré of November 27, 1830, shows the Blessed Mother standing on a globe with rays of light streaming from the jewels on her fingers. The Blessed Mother tells Catherine that these dazzling rays "are the symbols of the graces I shed upon those who ask for them." Mary also told St. Catherine that "the gems from which rays do not fall are the graces for which souls forget to ask."[9]

Fr. Joseph I. Dirwin, C.M., believes that the apparition of "the Virgin on the Globe" shows Mary "as the Mediatrix of all graces," which means that all graces "pass through her hands to mankind."[10] He also believes that the display on the back of the miraculous medal—which the Blessed Mother asked Catherine to have made—"is an obvious reference to Our Lady's part as Co-redemptress of the [human] race in the Sacred Hearts of Jesus and Mary."[11]

What is meant by "Mediatrix" and "Co-Redemptrix"?

The Marian titles of Mediatrix and Co-Redemptrix are related but distinct. The council fathers of Vatican II did not call Mary Co-Redemptrix,[12] but they did affirm her active cooperation in the work of redemption.

Lumen Gentium quotes St. Irenaeus, who notes that Mary, by her obedience to God's plan, "became the cause of salvation (*causa salutis*) for herself and for the whole human race" (*LG,* 56). Moreover, at the foot of the Cross, suffering in a profound way with her only-begotten Son, Mary "associated herself with a mother's heart with Christ's sacrifice" and lovingly consented "to the immolation of this victim which she herself had brought forth" (*LG,* 58). Thus, although Christ is the one Savior of the human race, Mary, by God's will, associated herself with his sacrificial offering in a unique and singular way. In this sense, she may be understood as the "Co-Redemptrix"—the one who cooperated in a unique and singular way with the Redeemer.[13]

Although Vatican II avoids calling Mary "Co-Redemptrix," it does speak of her as Mediatrix, recognizing Mary as worthy of invocation as "Advocate, Auxiliatrix (supporter), Adjutrix (helper) and Mediatrix" as long as these titles "in no way diminish or add to the dignity and efficacy of Christ the one Mediator" (*LG,* 62).

So, what does it mean, to call Mary "Mediatrix"? The word "mediation" comes from the Latin word *medius,* or "middle." The Latin verb *mediare* means to stand in the middle for the purpose of communication or reconciliation. In the Old Testament, priests, prophets, and kings serve as mediators between God and Israel.[14] In the New Testament, St. Paul tells us that the law "was promulgated by angels at the hand of a mediator" (Gal 3:19). This mediator (*mesites*) was Moses.

How, then, does this apply to Mary? In 1 Timothy 2:5–6 we are told "there is one mediator [*mesites*] between God and the human race, Christ Jesus, himself human, who gave himself as ransom for all." This verse speaks of Christ's unique mediation; it does not, however, preclude others from sharing in his work of mediation.

Lumen Gentium notes that "just as the priesthood of Christ is shared in various ways both by the ministers and by the faithful, and as the one goodness of God is really communicated in different ways to His creatures, so also the unique mediation of the Redeemer does not exclude but rather gives rise to a manifold cooperation which is but a sharing in this one source" (*LG*, 62). Mary's mediation of grace, therefore, is a participation in the mediation of Christ. Her role as Mediatrix emerges from the will of God rather than from some inner necessity.

Vatican II puts it this way: "The maternal duty of Mary toward men in no wise obscures or diminishes this unique mediation of Christ, but rather shows His power. For all the salvific influence of the Blessed Virgin on men originates, not from some inner necessity, but from the divine pleasure. It flows forth from the superabundance of the merits of Christ, rests on His mediation, depends entirely on it and draws all its power from it. In no way does it impede, but rather does it foster the immediate union of the faithful with Christ" (*LG*, 60).

How is this role of Mary as Mediatrix an extension of the role entrusted to her on earth?

Mary's role as Mediatrix is rooted in her divine maternity. As the Mother of the Word Incarnate, she served as the Mediatrix between the human race and its Savior. She received in her womb the Person of the Word of God, and she was the source of his human nature. Mary's role as Mediatrix is also manifested by her intercession as mother. St. John Paul II sees Mary's intercession at Cana as an expression of her maternal mediation:

> At Cana in Galilee there is shown only one concrete aspect of human need, apparently a small one of little importance ("They have no wine"). But it has a symbolic value: this coming to the aid of human needs means, at the same time, bringing those needs within the radius of Christ's messianic mission and salvific power. Thus there is a mediation: Mary places herself between her Son and mankind in the reality of their wants, needs and sufferings. She puts herself "in the middle," that is to say she acts as a mediatrix not as an outsider, but in her position as mother. She knows that as such she can point out to her Son the needs of mankind, and in fact, she "has the right" to do so. Her mediation is thus in the nature of intercession: Mary "intercedes" for mankind. And that is not all. As a mother she also wishes the messianic power of her Son to be manifested, that salvific power of his which is meant to help man in his misfortunes, to free him from the evil which in various forms and degrees weighs heavily upon his life. (*RM*, 21)

St. Bonaventure (ca. 1221–1274) identified three moments in the maternal mediation of Mary.[15] First, Mary saying yes to the invitation of God, which leads to her conceiving and begetting Christ, who would redeem the human race (see Luke 1:26–38). Second, Mary's union with Christ, when, at Calvary, he pays the price of redemption for the whole human race (see John 19:25–27). And finally, Mary's distribution of the fruits of Christ's redemption during the time of the Church: "For as through her, God came down to us, so it is right that through her we should ascend to God."[16]

How is Mary's role as Mediatrix supported by Magisterial teaching?

In his 1891 encyclical *Octobri mense*, Pope Leo XIII affirmed Mary as the Mediatrix of all graces:

> The Eternal Son of God, about to take upon Him our nature for the saving and ennobling of man, and about to consummate thus a mystical union between Himself and all mankind, did not accomplish His design without adding there the free consent of the elect Mother, who represented in some sort all human kind, according to the illustrious and just opinion of St. Thomas, who says that the Annunciation was effected with the consent of the Virgin standing in the place of humanity. With equal truth may it be also affirmed that, by the will of God, Mary is the intermediary through whom is distributed unto us this immense treasure of mercies gathered by God, for mercy and truth were created by Jesus Christ. Thus as no man goes to the Father but by the Son, so no man goes to Christ but by His Mother. (*OM*, 4)

In his 1904 encyclical, *Ad Diem Illum,* Pope Pius X affirmed Mary's role as the *dispensatrix* of all graces, teaching that Mary merited in a fitting manner (*de congruo*) the salvation that Christ merited in an absolute manner (*de condigno*):

> When the supreme hour of the Son came, beside the Cross of Jesus there stood Mary His Mother, . . . so entirely participating in His Passion, that if it had been possible she would have gladly borne all the torments that her Son bore.[17] And from this community of will and suffering between Christ and Mary she merited to become most worthily the Reparatrix of the lost world[18] and Dispensatrix of all the gifts that Our Savior purchased for us by His Death and by His Blood. (*ADI*, 12)

St. Pius X recognizes Mary's intimate association with Christ in the work of salvation as well as her active mediation of the graces merited by her divine Son. He makes it clear, though, that the Virgin Mary is not the source of the graces she helps to mediate. Quoting St. Bernadine of Siena, he explains:

> It cannot, of course, be denied that the dispensation of these treasures is the particular and peculiar right of Jesus Christ, for they are the exclusive fruit of His Death, who by His nature is the mediator between God and man. Nevertheless, by this companionship in sorrow and suffering already mentioned between the Mother and the Son, it has been allowed to the august Virgin to be the most powerful mediatrix and advocate of the whole world with her Divine Son (Pius IX. *Ineffabilis*). . . . Says St. Bernardine of Siena, "she is the neck of Our Head, by which He communicates to His mystical body all spiritual gifts."[19]
>
> We are then, it will be seen, very far from attributing to the Mother of God a productive power of grace—a power which belongs to God alone. Yet, since Mary carries it over all in holiness and union with Jesus Christ, and has been associated by Jesus Christ in the work of redemption, she merits for us *de congruo*, in the language of theologians, what Jesus Christ merits for us *de condigno*, and she is the supreme Minister of the distribution of graces.[20]

Is there reason to believe that at some point this title might be dogmatically defined, as was the title "Mother of God"?

During the first half of the twentieth century, there was a growing movement seeking to have a papal definition of Mary as Mediatrix of all graces. In 1921, Pope Benedict XV, in response to the request of Cardinal Mercier, approved the feast of Mary, Mediatrix of All Graces, for all the dioceses of Belgium and to all other dioceses and religious orders that wish to celebrate this feast.[21]

In 1945, Ida Peerdeman (1905–1996) claimed to receive the first of fifty-six apparitions of Mary, in which Mary identified

herself as Our Lady of All Nations (or "Peoples"), Co-Redemptrix, Mediatrix of All Graces, and Advocate.[22] According
to Peerdeman, the Lady of All Nations revealed that it is the
will of God that the pope dogmatically define the truth of these
three titles.[23] On May 31, 2002, Bishop J. M. Punt of Haarlam-
Amsterdam declared these apparitions worthy of belief as supernatural (though previous bishops of Amsterdam stated the
supernatural could not be verified).[24]

Efforts to have Mary formally proclaimed Mediatrix of
all graces or Co-Redemptrix have not been realized. All the
popes from Leo XIII through John XXIII referred to Mary as
the Mediatrix of all graces, but they stopped short of defining
this dogmatically.[25]

In its 1962 Marian *schema*, Vatican II called Mary "Mediatrix of all graces," though *Lumen Gentium* refers to her simply
as "Mediatrix" (*LG*, 62). St. John Paul II, however, explicitly
referred to Mary as the Mediatrix of all graces on six separate
occasions.[26]

Pope Benedict XVI in his May 11, 2007, homily for the
canonization of St. Antonio de Sant'ana de Galvão, O.F.M.,
affirmed Mary as the Mediatrix of all graces without using the
term when he said: "There is no fruit of grace in the history of
salvation that does not have as its necessary instrument the
mediation of Our Lady."[27] Benedict XVI did, however, refer to
Mary as "the Mediatrix of all graces" in a letter dated January
10, 2013, to Archbishop Zimowski as the papal representative
to the World Day of the Sick. In this letter, he entrusts the mission of the archbishop to "the Blessed Immaculate Virgin Mary,
the Mediatrix of all graces" (*Beatae Virginis Mariae Immaculatae,
Mediatricis omnium gratiarum*).[28]

The Blessed Mother is recognized as the Mediatrix of
all graces by multiple popes in their ordinary Magisterium.
Although not formally defined as a dogma, it is a teaching
that enjoys much support and is certainly worthy of belief.
The 1830 apparitions of the Blessed Mother to St. Catherine
Labouré provide the support of an approved private revelation

for Mary's role as the Mediatrix of all graces. Just as the Word of God came to us through the mediation of Mary, it seems only fitting that the graces of the Savior come to us through her maternal mediation. In the words of Vatican II, Mary "is our Mother in the order of grace" (*LG*, 61).

◇◇◇

PRAYER TO OUR LADY OF THE MIRACULOUS MEDAL ⚜

Virgin Mother of God, Mary Immaculate, I unite myself to you under the title of Our Lady of the Miraculous Medal.

May this medal be a sure sign of your motherly affection, and a constant reminder of my filial duties to you.

While I am wearing it, bless me by your loving protection and preserve me in the grace of your Son.

Most powerful Virgin, mother of our Savior, keep me close to you at every moment so that, like you, I may live and act according to the teaching and example of your Son.

Obtain for me the grace of a happy death, so that in union with you and your Son, I may enjoy the happiness of heaven forever. Amen.

Mary as Advocate:
Our Lady of Pontmain

"Mother of Hope, of name so sweet, protect our country, pray for us, pray for us!" During this singing, the Blessed Virgin lifted her hands to the height of her shoulders . . . and moved her fingers lightly as if she were accompanying the singing of the hymn.

At the feet of the vision of Our Lady were traced in the sky the words: "But pray my children, God will hear you in a short time." And a short time afterwards, indeed only ten days later, the armistice was signed. . . . It was the prelude to forty years of peace.

ABBÉ M. RICHARD[1]

Throughout Christian history, the Mother of God has interceded for her children as an advocate in times of war, famine, plague, and natural disaster. The abrupt end of the war through the appearance of Mary as Our Lady of Hope at Pontmain, France, is perhaps the clearest example of this maternal protection and advocacy.

The apparition of Our Lady of Pontmain occured in the context of the Franco-Prussian War. At the beginning of 1871, the outlook for France was bleak. Paris was under siege, French

armies were defeated, and Metz—perhaps the most important fortress in all of Europe—had been besieged the previous
August and had to surrender by October. The people of Paris
were starving. The Second Empire had fallen, and the Prussian
and Allied troops had started to occupy a large portion of the
French territory.

And so, on January 12, 1871, the Prussians advanced west-
ward toward the Mayenne. The local people—ravaged by
typhoid, smallpox, and unrelenting hunger—fearfully turned
in desperation to God, begging to be spared the suffering of
war.

Their prayers were answered in a most miraculous way.

Pontmain, France, 1871

Throughout the evening of January 17, 1871, snow had fallen
and covered the village of Pontmain. Two young boys, twelve-
year-old Eugene and ten-year-old Joseph Barbedette, helped
their father with yardwork and disposing of the weeds in their
family's barn. Pausing from his work for a moment, Eugene
looked out a window and saw a woman. Calmly he asked the
others nearby—his father, his brother, and a visiting woman—
if they could see her, but they could not. He described her to
them. Then his father sent Eugene to the house to fetch his
mother. Joseph took that opportunity to go outside to look for
himself, and when he saw the woman, he clapped his hands
and shouted, "Oh how beautiful she is! Oh how beautiful she
is!" His shout brought the others running.[2]

A neighbor boy, who had heard the shout, came running
and saw the vision, but the adults could see nothing. Soon other
villagers came running as well as the other children from the
nearby convent school. All the children also saw the "beautiful,
tall Lady." The vision was not perceptible to the nearby adults,
but when Françoise Richer (eleven), Jeanne-Marie Lebossé
(nine), and Eugene Friteau (six) all claimed to see the woman,

Sr. Marie Edward began to lead the crowd that had formed in prayer.

"The Lady is the same size as Sister Vitaline!"[3]

The children were in absolute agreement over what they had seen: The Virgin Mary wore a blue robe decorated with golden stars. On her head was a black veil and a gold crown, and on her feet were blue shoes with gold ribbons. She was tall and beautiful, like the children's favorite teacher, and looked about eighteen years old. When the large cross with a bloody Christ appeared in her hands, the children suddenly became sad and explained that the face of the Virgin had become sad too. One of the visionaries, Joseph Barbedette, recalled that "her face was marked with a deep sorrow . . . the trembling of her lips at the corners of her mouth showed deep feeling. . . . But no tears ran down her cheeks."[4]

Like the famous vision of Our Lady of Knock, which would occur eight years later in Ireland, the apparition was motionless at first. After two hours, as the crowd prayed the Rosary, some motion began to take place with different elements in the scene beginning to animate. A small red cross appeared over the heart of the vision, and a blue oval frame with four candles appeared around her and seemed to get lit one-by-one by one of the stars. The stars on her robe began to grow brighter.

As the crowd began to pray the Magnificat, she elevated her hands with the palms outward. And as the priest began singing the *Ave Maris Stella*, the Lady lowered her hands, and two white crosses appeared on her shoulders. She stayed until the parish priest began to lead the prayer; at that time a white veil rose from below her and covered her until she disappeared.

The Message of Mary

There had been no verbal message imparted to the children. Instead, a white banner with golden text appeared under the Lady's feet: "But pray, my children. God will soon grant your request." The larger cross in her hands had a banner bearing the name of Christ hanging down from it. Then a second statement appeared: "My Son allows himself to be moved."

On the night of the apparition to the children at 5:30 p.m., the Prussian army stopped its march through France when the Prussian commander claimed to have experienced the presence of the Virgin Mary. General Schmidt reported, "We cannot go any further. Yonder, in the direction of Brittany, there is an invisible Madonna barring the way."[5]

General Chanzy, commander of the Place de Laval, received the testimony of the German delegation, which described a beautiful lady who had appeared to them in the sky on January 17, 1871, around 5:45 p.m.: "She wore a blue dress studded with gold stars, a black veil on her head hiding her hair, an inverted golden cone, and half a red border, and she stood between you and us, and we were pushed back with the palms of her hands, and then we felt a burning fire that precipitated our departure. This lady protects you, and she pursued our troops, who had to run."[6]

A peace treaty between France and Prussia was signed ten days later. All the soldiers from Pontmain returned home unharmed. The inhabitants of Pontmain and the surrounding area had been spared, especially since the Prussians did not enter Laval. Later the visionaries Joseph and Eugene Barbadette entered the seminary and became priests. Françoise Richer became housekeeper for Abbot Eugene Barbedette, and Jeanne-Marie Lebossé entered the convent.

The Church Responds

Msgr. Casimir-Alexis-Joseph Wicart, bishop of Laval, quickly ordered an investigation into the events and travelled to Pontmain to personally question people. Further inquiry followed to determine the veracity of the apparition.

On February 2, 1872, the bishop of Laval released a statement of approval of the apparition: "We judge that the

Immaculate Mary, Mother of God, has truly appeared on January 17, 1871, to Eugene Barbedette, Joseph Barbedette, Françoise Richer, and Jeanne-Marie Lebossé, in the hamlet of Pontmain." In the same proclamation he recognized the authenticity of the apparition, approved the cult of Our Lady of Hope of Pontmain, and called for the building of a sanctuary that was completed in 1890 and dedicated a decade later. The bishop also called the Missionary Oblates of Mary Immaculate to organize the first pilgrimages and to spread the devotion to Our Lady of Pontmain in the region. For the first anniversary of the apparition, January 17, 1872, there were already eight thousand people who arrived on pilgrimage. Today an average of two hundred fifty thousand pilgrims arrive at Pontmain each year.[7]

According to the most recent Church document about the process of validation, from the Sacred Congregation for the Doctrine of the Faith in its 1978 *Norms Regarding the Manner of Proceeding in the Discernment of Presumed Apparitions or Revelations*, there does not need to be an extra public action from the Vatican to certify or ratify a local bishop's approval. The local ordinary is the main authority in judging apparition cases.

However, in rare cases, Rome will show signs of support and recognition for a supernatural event that reinforce its validity and establish its importance for the universal Church. The apparition at Pontmain is one of these cases. The following are signs of papal recognition for the events at Pontmain:

- In 1905, Pope Pius X elevated the sanctuary to the status of a basilica. In September 1908, the Basilica of Our Lady of Hope of Pontmain was solemnly dedicated in the presence of two archbishops, four bishops, six hundred priests, and 1,500 pilgrims.
- In 1932, Pope Pius XI confirmed the decision of the bishop and granted a Mass and Office proper to Our Lady of Hope of Pontmain.

- On July 16, 1932, the future Pope Pius XII (then Cardinal Pacelli) passed a decree from the Chapter of St. Peter's Basilica that the statue of the Mother of Hope be solemnly honored with a crown of gold. On July 24, 1934, the statue of Our Lady was crowned in the presence of the archbishop, bishops, priests, and the laity by Cardinal Verdier, archbishop of Paris.
- In 1946, the seventy-fifth anniversary Mass was presided over by the apostolic nuncio Monsignor Angelo Giuseppe Roncalli, the future Pope John XXIII.

Mary as "Advocate" in Scripture and throughout Church History

by Dr. Robert Fastiggi

In the January 17, 1871, apparition at Pontmain, France, the Blessed Mother revealed herself as "the Mother of Hope" (*Mère de l'Espérance*) because she interceded for the French, who were facing defeat during the Franco-Prussian War. Not only did the Blessed Mother appear to four children at Pontmain; she also made her presence felt to General Schmidt, the commander of the Prussian army, who stated that "an invisible Madonna" was barring the way for the advance of his forces toward Brittany in France. A few weeks after the January 17, 1871, apparition at Pontmain, an armistice was signed that paved the way for the cessation of the war.

In the vision of the four children at Pontmain, two messages appeared in writing beneath Our Lady's feet. The first was, "But pray, my children. God will soon grant your request"

(*Mais priez mes enfants. Dieu vous exaucera en peu de temps*). The second message was "My Son allows himself to be moved" (*Mon fils se laisse toucher*). These two messages show that prayers can move God to intervene in earthly affairs. They also show how the Blessed Mother advocates for those in need.

How is Mary an advocate?

An advocate is a person called to defend or strengthen the position of someone in need. The word comes from the Latin *ad vocare*, which means "to call to" or "to summon." The Greek word for "advocate" is *parákletos*, which is the name given by Jesus to the Holy Spirit (see John 14:16, 26). The Holy Spirit is the *Parákletos* because he intercedes on our behalf and provides comfort and strength to us when we are in need. Jesus, though, is also called *Parákletos* in 1 John 2:1 because he is "the righteous one" who is our advocate with the Father.

If the Holy Spirit and Jesus are our advocates, how can Mary also be our advocate? The answer is found in scripture, which asks that "supplications, prayers, petitions, and thanksgivings be offered for everyone, for kings and for all in authority, that we may lead a quiet and tranquil life in all devotion and dignity" (1 Tm 2:1–2). If we can intercede in prayer for the needs of others, how much more can the Mother of God, who revealed her intercessory power at the wedding feast of Cana (see John 2:1–12)? The apparition of Mary at Pontmain makes clear that Jesus allows himself to be moved by prayer.

Lumen Gentium refers to Mary as Advocate along with other titles such as Mediatrix and Auxiliatrix. These titles are appropriate because Mary "by her maternal charity . . . cares for the brethren of her Son, who still journey on earth surrounded by dangers and difficulties, until they are led to the happiness of their true home" (*LG*, 62). These titles, however, do not take away "anything to the dignity and efficaciousness of Christ the one Mediator." Mary, therefore, shares in the work of advocacy and mediation with and under her divine Son in communion with the Holy Spirit.

Where do we find Mary as advocate in scripture and tradition?

Mary shows herself to be an advocate for the wedding guests at Cana (see John 2), although she is not directly given the title "advocate" in scripture. In the early Church, however, St. Irenaeus (ca. 130–202) recognized Mary as the "New Eve" who became "the advocate (*advocata*) of the virgin Eve."[8] St. Irenaeus's reference to Mary as advocate represents "the first time in the history of ancient Christian literature that this title is used for Mary."[9] Unfortunately, we no longer have the original Greek of the entire *Adverses haereses* of Irenaeus; however, the Armenian version "seems to indicate that the original Greek word was *parákletos* (defender, advocate, intercessor)."[10]

Other Church Fathers also referred to Mary as advocate. St. Ephrem the Syrian (ca. 306–373) spoke of Mary as "the advocate of the abandoned."[11] St. Romanus the Singer (ca. 490–556) depicted Mary addressing Adam and Eve after the fall saying: "Cease your lamentations; I shall be your advocate with my son."[12] Theoteknos of Livias (ca. 550–650) called Mary "the advocate of the human race."[13] St. John of Damascus (ca. 675–749), in his second Sermon on the Dormition, referred to the Blessed Mother as *Paraclesis*—which is related to *Parákletos*, but is usually translated as "consolation."[14]

The ancient prayer to Mary, the *Sub tuum praesidium*—which dates from the third or fourth century—affirms Mary as our advocate implicitly as well. The prayer reads: "We fly to thy protection, O Holy Mother of God. Do not despise our petitions in our necessities, but deliver us always from all dangers, O Glorious and Blessed Virgin."[15] The prayer recognizes Mary's role as intercessor and advocate. It sees her as "a source of protection in the face of life's trials and temptations."[16]

In the Latin West, the term "advocate" was used more broadly. St. Augustine, for example, spoke of the martyrs as our advocates (*advocati*) who share in the ministry of Christ the Advocate.[17] If the martyrs can serve as our advocates, then certainly the Mother of God can as well.

The Salve Regina *mentions Mary as advocate. What are the origins of this prayer?*

The Marian antiphon known as the *Salve Regina* ("Hail, Holy Queen") was composed during this early Middle Ages, when there was a particular emphasis on this aspect of Mary's role as advocate.[18] Around 1135, the Abbey of Cluny began using the *Salve Regina* in its liturgical services. By the thirteenth century, many religious communities, such as the Dominicans, were using it, and in the fourteenth century it was included in the Divine Office.[19]

The prayer reads as follows:

> Hail, holy Queen, Mother of Mercy; hail our life, our sweetness and our hope. To thee do we cry, poor banished children of Eve. To thee do we send up our sighs, mourning and weeping in this valley of tears. Turn, then, most gracious advocate, thine eyes of mercy toward us; and after this, our exile, show unto us the blessed fruit of thy womb, Jesus. O clement, O loving, O sweet Virgin Mary.[20]

In this prayer, Mary is referred to as "most gracious advocate" (*advocata nostra*). As advocate, Mary intercedes as our spiritual mother from heaven. As our Mother of Mercy, she comes to our assistance out of mercy toward us. She also helps to mediate the Divine Mercy of her Son as "our Mother in the order of grace" (*LG*, 61).

Due in part to the widespread use of the *Salve Regina*, references to Mary as advocate became common after this period. St. Bernard of Clairvaux (1090–1153), in his second sermon for Advent, called upon Mary saying, "Our Lady, our Mediatress, our Advocate (*Advocata*), reconcile us to your Son, commend us to your Son, represent us before your Son."[21]

What do more recent popes teach about Mary as advocate?

Many popes since the sixteenth century have referred to Mary as "Advocate," including Leo X (1520), Sixtus V (1587), Clement IX (1667), and Clement XI (1708).[22] In his 1805 apostolic constitution, *Tanto studio*, Pope Pius VII explains why Mary's power of intercession as our advocate is more powerful than that of the other saints:

> For, while the prayers of those in heaven have, it is true, some claim on God's watchful eye, Mary's prayers place their assurance in a mother's right. For that reason, when she approaches her divine Son's throne, as advocate she begs, as handmaid she prays, but as Mother she commands.[23]

Pope Pius X speaks of Mary as "our Queen and Advocate" in his 1903 prayer, *Virgine Sanctissima*.[24] In his 1928 encyclical, *Miserentissimus Redemptor*, Pope Pius XI says that Christ our Lord, "though the sole Mediator between God and man, wished to make His mother the advocate of sinners and the dispenser and mediatrix of His grace."[25] And in his October 12, 1947, radio message to the National Marian Congress of Argentina, Pope Pius XII quotes the Jesuit Francisco Suárez (1548–1617): "We have the Virgin as universal advocate in all things, for she is more powerful in whatever necessity than are all the other saints in particular needs."[26]

The Vatican II, as we have seen, affirmed Mary as advocate in *Lumen Gentium*. The council also taught that Mary's maternal intercession will last "until the eternal fulfillment of all the elect" (*LG*, 62).

Pope John Paul II also affirmed the Blessed Mother as the most powerful intercessor and advocate under God: "Mary is always at the very center of our prayer. She is the first among those who ask. She is the *Omnipotentia supplex*: the Omnipotence of intercession."[27] In his 1987 encyclical, *Redemptoris Mater*, John Paul II links Mary's role as advocate with her spiritual maternity. He notes that "throughout her life, the Church maintains with the Mother of God a link which embraces, in the saving mystery, the past, the present and the future, and venerates her as the spiritual mother of humanity and the advocate of grace" (47). In his General Audience of September 24, 1997, John Paul II explains how Mary as advocate cooperates with the Holy Spirit and with Christ:

> The title "Advocate" goes back to St. Irenaeus. With regard to Eve's disobedience and Mary's obedience, he says that at the moment of the Annunciation "the Virgin Mary became the Advocate" of Eve (*Haer.* 5, 19, 1; *PG* 7, 1175–1176). In fact, with her "yes" she defended our first mother and freed her from the consequences of her disobedience, becoming the cause of salvation for her and the whole human race.
>
> Mary exercises her role as "Advocate" by co-operating both with the Spirit the Paraclete and with the One who interceded on the Cross for his persecutors (cf. Lk 23:34), whom John calls our "advocate with the Father" (1 Jn 2:1). As a mother, she defends her children and protects them from the harm caused by their own sins. Christians call upon Mary as "Helper," recognizing her motherly love which sees her children's needs and is ready to come to their aid, especially when their eternal salvation is at stake.[28]

When Our Lady appeared to the four children at Pontmain in 1871, she was acting as advocate for the French people who were praying for the end of the Franco-Prussian War. She made it clear that her Son "allows himself to be moved" by prayer. As our spiritual mother and advocate, Mary joins her prayers to ours with a special power. As St. John Paul II has said, "She is the *Omnipotentia supplex*: the Omnipotence of intercession."

◇◇◇

PRAYER TO OUR LADY OF HOPE ⚜

O Mary, my mother, I kneel before you with heavy heart. The burden of my sins oppresses me. The knowledge of my weakness discourages me. I am beset by fears and temptations of every sort. Yet I am so attached to the things of this world that instead of longing for heaven I am filled with dread at the thought of death.

O Mother of Mercy, have pity on me in my distress. You are all-powerful with your Divine Son. He can refuse no request of your Immaculate Heart. Show yourself a true mother to me by being my advocate before his throne. O Refuge of Sinners and Hope of the Hopeless, to whom shall I turn if not to you?

Obtain for me, then, O Mother of Hope, the grace of true sorrow for my sins, the gift of perfect resignation to God's holy will, and the courage to take up my cross and follow Jesus. . . . Hope of the Hopeless, pray for us. Amen.

Adapted from the NOVENA TO OUR LADY OF HOPE[29]

CHAPTER 8

Mary as Mother of Mercy: Our Lady of Banneux

Believe in me and I will believe in you. . . . My dear child, pray, pray very much.
OUR LADY OF BANNEUX to Mariette Beco

The apparitions of Banneux invite Christians to question themselves about the mystery of suffering, which finds its meaning in the mystery of the Cross of the Lord. . . . Every person who offers his suffering contributes mysteriously to raising the world to God, and shares especially in the work of our redemption.
POPE JOHN PAUL II to the Most Reverend Albert Hossiau,
Bishop of Liège
July 31, 1999 [1]

In his pastoral letter to the bishop of Liège, written fifty years after the 1949 approval of the apparitions at Banneux, Pope John Paul II recalled his apostolic visit in 1985 to honor "Our Lady of the Poor, Health of the Sick."[2] It was there that the Blessed Mother showed eleven-year-old Mariette Beco a spring "reserved for all nations . . . to relieve the sick."[3] Eight separate times between January and March 1933, Our Lady appeared to

the girl to "alleviate sufferings" and to urge the young visionary to pray.

In doing so, Mary showed herself as "Mother of Mercy"
not only concerning the physical weaknesses that so often
afflict and beset us but also our spiritual weaknesses as well.
As the pope observed in his letter, "With Mary we become
humble children in the Lord's hands, asking forgiveness for our
faults and thereby discovering the joy of being God's children
who know they are infinitely loved and so have a deep desire
to be converted" (4).

Banneux, Belgium, 1933

Seventy-five years had passed since Our Lady of Lourdes had
appeared to young Bernadette Soubirous and showed her a
healing spring. This time she appeared in Belgium, to eleven-
year-old Mariette Beco, in a garden behind the Beco family's
cottage. Calling herself the "Virgin of the Poor," the Blessed
Mother promised to intercede for the poor, the sick, and the
suffering, thus showing herself to be the "Mother of Mercy."

This was a family sorely in need of such mercy. Mariette
was the oldest child of seven in a working family of nonpracticing Catholics. They lived in a house on the plateau of the
Ardennes. Neither her out-of-work wiremaker father, Julian,
nor her mother, Louise, was very devout, and Mariette had
missed Mass for two months and was underperforming in
catechism class. She no longer received instruction for Holy
Communion. And yet, it was to her that the Blessed Mother
entrusted this message of mercy to the poor, the sick, and the
ignorant—those who most needed the mercy of God.

On January 15, 1933, Mariette saw something illuminated
outside her window. Thinking it might be the reflection of her
oil lamp, she transferred the lamp to another room and looked
more carefully. Through the window she saw an illuminated,
beautiful woman holding a rosary in her hands.

In her account of her vision, Mariette saw the Virgin surrounded by a "great oval light," wearing a long, white gown with a sash of "unforgettable blue" and a white, transparent veil covering her head and shoulders. She was barefoot in the snow but did not appear cold, and her right foot was visible, "crowned with a golden rose" between the toes. She had a rosary on her right arm with beads sparkling like diamonds and a golden chain and cross. As in many other apparitions of Mary, she stood on a cloud.

Mariette's mother thought that perhaps she had seen something fleeting, but she was incredulous of her daughter's story. She locked the door and prohibited her from trying to see anything more of the vision. Mariette and a friend at school wanted to relate the story to the parish priest, Fr. Louis Jamin, but he accused her of trying to be a copycat of the Beauraing apparitions, which had occurred about fifty miles southwest of their village between 1932 and 1933. When over the next few days the Virgin did not appear again, Mariette decided to restart her catechism classes. Her piety and mastery of the material surprised Fr. Jamin, who encouraged her to seek the guidance of the Virgin Mary.

The Messages of Mary

On January 18 at 7:00 p.m., Mariette went to the back of the house, got on her knees, and began to pray silently. This was not typical for his daughter, so her father and two neighbors came to see what was going on.

Mariette told her father that she had witnessed a giant orb of blinding light passing through the forest. It grew in size and advanced to right in front of her, eventually transforming into a "woman's silhouette" resting on a cloud. Mariette shouted, "She is calling me!" and getting quickly to her feet, sprinted toward the road. She abruptly stopped, however, and knelt near a spring. Later, she explained that she had heard the Virgin say, "Plunge your hands in the water! This fountain is reserved for me. Goodnight. Goodbye." Quickly her form became a ball of light that disappeared into the horizon.

Later that evening at around 10:00 p.m., Fr. Jamin went to the Becos' house and listened to Julian's account of what happened. The priest marveled at the man's unexpected conversion, immediately expressing his desire to make a general confession and go to Mass.

Word began to spread around the small village about the apparitions. The following day at the same time, Mariette began to pray the Rosary with seventeen people around her. When the Virgin appeared for the third time, Mariette asked her who she was, and the Lady said, "I am the Virgin of the Poor." Then, standing with her at the spring, the Lady announced, "This spring is reserved for all the nations, to bring comfort to the sick." Finally, she comforted Mariette with these words before departing: "I will pray for you; goodbye." Again she vanished in a ball of light.

The next day, January 20, at around 6:45 p.m., Fr. Jamin and two journalists joined eleven other witnesses for the fourth apparition. This time, the Virgin made a request that is often heard in testimonies of apparitions: "I would like a small chapel." When the Virgin traced the Sign of the Cross over Mariette's forehead, the girl lost consciousness.

To Mariette's surprise, for the next few weeks the apparitions stopped, prompting people to ridicule her and mock her with the name "St. Bernadette."

She continued going out in the cold and praying, believing that the Virgin would return. On the feast of Our Lady of Lourdes, February 11, at 7 p.m., the Virgin made her fifth appearance. Mariette ran with abandon toward her and fell into the spring to place her rosary in the water. Mary reminded her, "I come to alleviate sufferings."

The next day, Mariette received her First Communion from Fr. Jamin.

Several days later, on the fifteenth and again on the twentieth, Mariette saw the Virgin Mary again as she recited the Rosary. The Virgin encouraged her to "pray very much."

On March 2, 1933, the Virgin appeared for the eighth and final time and identified herself: "I am the Mother of the Savior, the Mother of God." Again she urged Mariette: "Pray very much." Then she placed her hands on Mariette's head and blessed her with the Sign of the Cross, saying, "Adieu. Till we meet in God." Mariette tearfully recognized that this would be the final time the Virgin would appear to her.

After the apparitions ceased, Mariette sought privacy. She got married and led a quiet family life. In 2008, the year of the official ceremonies of the seventy-fifth anniversary of the apparitions, she asked the rector of the shrine to publish a letter in which she gave a final reflection on her role in the apparitions: "I was no more than a postal worker who delivers the mail. Once this has been done, the postman is of no importance anymore." On December 2, 2011, Mariette Beco passed away at the age of ninety in the Home de la Vierge des Pauvres at Banneux.

The Visions Are Investigated

In an initial show of support for the visions, Fr. Jamin honored the request of the Virgin, and a little chapel was built and inaugurated. Today, the small spring nearby, which the Virgin showed to Mariette, yields about two thousand gallons of water a day, with many reports of miraculous healings.

On March 19, 1935, an episcopal commission headed by Msgr. Leroux, director of the diocesan major seminary, began an investigation of the purported apparitions. They interviewed seventy-three people, testifying under oath. By February of 1937, the commission's work was finished and was transmitted by the diocese of Liège to the archbishop of Brussels-Mechlin and then to Rome.[4]

Five years later in May 1942, the bishop, Msgr. Louis-Joseph Kerkhofs of Liège, promulgated full and entire authorization for practicing the "cultus" (up to that point devotion had been merely tolerated because of the proliferation of "copycat" visions). Cardinal Van Roy, primate of Belgium, had been actively intervening to exclude any devotion or potential approval of any apparitions reported within his jurisdiction except for those at Beauraing and Banneux, which were being examined by their respective bishops (Namur and Liège).

On June 19, 1942, a committee was assembled to make a pronouncement on the reliability of the seer and on the purported supernatural character of the apparitions. Some assessments considered her "hysterical." Others wondered about a potential deception at play or a dramatization of the imagination of Mariette: who perhaps had some knowledge of the visions experienced by St. Bernadette. In its final meeting, February 15, 1944, the committee remained dubious about what had transpired: "The events of Banneux appear to be neither certain nor even probable."[5]

The following year, Msgr. Kerkhofs, with the help of Fr. Rene Rutten, S.J. (1878–1948), ordered a third and final investigation committee. This time, the conclusions were positive, and on August 22, 1949, sixteen years after the events, their supernatural origin was officially recognized with the support of the Vatican. Msgr. Kerkhofs, bishop of Liège, gave his approval: "Two times, first in 1942 and then in 1947, we have officially recognized the reality of the apparitions of Banneux. Today after two new years of prayer and observation, we believe in conscience to be able and to be required to recognize without reserve this reality, namely, the reality of the eight apparitions of the Holy Virgin to Mariette Beco."[6]

Over the years the Vatican has shown its support for the authenticity of these apparitions in various ways. On August 14, 1956, Msgr. E. Forni, the apostolic nuncio to Brussels, solemnly crowned the statue of the Virgin of the Poor. In 1985, Pope John Paul II went to Banneux and had an audience with Mariette at the sacristy. More than a decade later, on July 31, 1999, the Vatican issued a letter to the bishop of Liège to commemorate the fiftieth anniversary of the approval of the apparitions; similarly, on May 31, 2008, the Vatican sent a special envoy from Pope Benedict XVI to the celebrations marking the seventy-fifth anniversary of the apparitions of the Virgin of the Poor.

The feast of Our Lady of Banneux is observed on January 15.

Mary as "Mother of Mercy" in Scripture and throughout Church History
by Dr. Robert Fastiggi

When the Blessed Virgin Mary appeared to Mariette Beco at Banneux in 1933, she revealed herself as "the Virgin of the Poor." She told Mariette that the spring near her house would be reserved for all nations to bring comfort to the sick. She also said to Mariette: "I come to relieve suffering" (*je viens soulager la souffrance*)."[7] To relieve the suffering of the poor and the sick is an act of mercy. This is why Our Lady of Banneux can be understood as both the Mother of Mercy and the Virgin of the Poor.

What does the Bible say about mercy?

Mercy is one of the great attributes of God. In the Old Testament, the word for mercy is *hesed*, which refers to God's goodness and loving-kindness, especially in forgiving sin.[8] In Mary's prayer, the Magnificat, she proclaims that God's "mercy is from age to age to those who fear him" (Lk 1:50). The Canticle of Zechariah likewise says that the Lord God of Israel has "visited and brought redemption to his people" and promised "to show mercy to our fathers and to be mindful of his holy covenant" (Lk 1:68–72).

God's mercy is revealed most clearly in the person of Jesus Christ, who said to Philip, "Whoever has seen me has seen the Father" (Jn 14:9). Throughout the gospels, we see the merciful hand of Jesus, who healed the sick, raised the dead, and converted hearts. Therefore, it is only right that, just as Mary is "Mother of God," she is also "Mother of Mercy." Mary's identity as the Mother of Mercy is grounded in sacred scripture, especially by her presence under the Cross (see John 19:25–27) and her mercy shown at the wedding feast of Cana (see John 2:1–10).

How is the title "Virgin of the Poor" tied to "Mother of Mercy"?

The mercy shown by Our Lady of Banneux is not only toward those who are materially poor and physically sick. As Robert Maloy, S.M., explains: "Mary is the 'Virgin of the Poor' because she is always trying to help us out of the poverty of sin, the cramped corners of self-love, the dingy desolation of sensuality."[9]

Mary's love for sinners is an expression of her identity as the Mother of Mercy. Vatican II teaches that Mary's merciful love for sinners "lasts until the eternal fulfillment of all the elect" (LG, 62). After her Assumption into heaven, Mary did not lay aside this salvific duty, but by her constant intercession she continues to bring us the gifts of eternal salvation. Mary is also "the model of virtues" and the model of the Beatitudes (LG, 65). In the Sermon on the Mount, Jesus tells us: "Blessed are the merciful, for they will be shown mercy" (Mt 5:7). The Blessed Mother's love for the poor, the sick, and the sinful is an expression of this Beatitude.

How did Mary experience God's mercy, since she was free of sin?

Mary herself received God's mercy from the first moment of her conception. As Pope John Paul II teaches:

> Mary is also the one who obtained mercy in a particular and exceptional way, as no other person has. At the same time, still in an exceptional way, she made possible with the sacrifice of her heart her own sharing in revealing God's mercy. This sacrifice is intimately linked with the cross of her Son, at the foot of which she was to stand on Calvary. Her sacrifice is a unique sharing in the revelation of mercy, that is, a sharing in the absolute fidelity of God to His own love, to the covenant that He willed from eternity and that He entered into in time with man, with the people, with humanity. (*Dives in Misericordia*, 9)

The Passion and Death of Jesus on the Cross is the deepest revelation of God's merciful love. Pope Benedict XVI described Jesus as "the incarnate love of God."[10] This love was expressed in dramatic fashion on Calvary, and Mary participated in the mystery of the Cross in a preeminent manner. Pope John Paul II put it this way:

> No one has experienced, to the same degree as the Mother of the crucified One, the mystery of the cross, the overwhelming encounter of divine transcendent justice with love: that "kiss" given by mercy to justice. No one has received into his heart, as much as Mary did, that mystery, that truly divine dimension of the redemption effected on Calvary by means of the death of the Son, together with the sacrifice of her maternal heart, together with her definitive "fiat."
>
> Mary, then, is the one who has the deepest knowledge of the mystery of God's mercy. She knows its price; she knows how great it is. In this sense, we call her the Mother of mercy: our Lady of mercy, or Mother of divine mercy; in

each one of these titles there is a deep theological meaning, for they express the special preparation of her soul, of her whole personality, so that she was able to perceive, through the complex events, first of Israel, then of every individual and of the whole of humanity, that mercy of which "from generation to generation" people become sharers according to the eternal design of the most Holy Trinity. (*DM*, 9)

How has the title Mother of Mercy been recognized in the liturgical and devotional life of the Church?

Various Church Fathers recognized Mary as a source of mercy. St. Ephrem of Syria (ca. 306–373) referred to the Blessed Virgin as "the inexhaustible fount of mercy." In one of his sermons, St. Jacob of Sarug (ca. 451–521) called her the "Mother of Mercy," and St. Sophronius (ca. 560–639) extolled Mary as "the abyss of mercy."[11] The Akathist Hymn says, "Let every hymn yield which seeks to match your infinite mercy."[12] In a sermon attributed to St. Augustine (354–430), Mary is called "the most merciful (*misericordissima*)."[13]

The title Mother of Mercy was promoted in a special way by St. Odo (ca. 880–942), the Abbot of Cluny (cf. *Vita Odonis* I:9: PL 133:47).[14] The title was given added popularity by the Marian hymn the *Salve Regina* or the "Hail Holy Queen," which refers to the "Mother of mercy."

Various popes, such as Gregory IX (ca. 1145–1241) and St. Pius V (ca. 1504–1572), decreed that the Marian hymn *Salve Regina* be chanted or sung after Compline or Vespers during certain times of the liturgical year.[15] The liturgical use of the title led to references to Mary as Mother of Mercy by saints such as St. Bridget of Sweden (1303–1373), St. Lawrence of Brindisi (1559–1619), and St. Alphonsus Liguori (1696–1787).[16] St. Lawrence of Brindisi says the Blessed Virgin is "the most merciful, the most compassionate mother, the most tender mother, the most loving mother."[17] Numerous popes have also called Mary "the Mother of Mercy," such as Leo XIII (1810–1903), St. Pius X (1835–1914), and Benedict XV (1854–1922).[18]

Mary's role as Mother of Mercy is closely linked to her intercessions as our spiritual mother from heaven. As our Mother of Mercy, she comes to our assistance and helps to mediate the Divine Mercy of her son. In her *Diary*, St. Faustina Kowalska (1905–1938) told of a vision she had of the Mother of God with the Infant Jesus in her arms. The Blessed Mother told Faustina: "I am not only the Queen of Heaven, but the Mother of Mercy and your Mother."[19]

Mary's identity as our "Mother of Mercy" is beautifully summarized by Pope Francis in his April 11, 2015, Bull of Indiction, *Misericordiae Vultus,* for the Extraordinary Jubilee of Mercy:

> My thoughts now turn to the Mother of Mercy. May the sweetness of her countenance watch over us in this Holy Year, so that all of us may rediscover the joy of God's tenderness. No one has penetrated the profound mystery of the incarnation like Mary. Her entire life was patterned after the presence of mercy made flesh. The Mother of the Crucified and Risen One has entered the sanctuary of divine mercy because she participated intimately in the mystery of His love.
>
> Chosen to be the Mother of the Son of God, Mary, from the outset, was prepared by the love of God to be the *Ark of the Covenant* between God and man. She treasured divine mercy in her heart in perfect harmony with her Son Jesus. Her hymn of praise, sung at the threshold of the home of Elizabeth, was dedicated to the mercy of God which extends from "generation to generation" (*Lk* 1:50). We too were included in those prophetic words of the Virgin Mary. This will be a source of comfort and strength to us as we cross the threshold of the Holy Year to experience the fruits of divine mercy. (*MV*, 24)

Like St. John Paul II, Pope Francis points to Mary's presence under the Cross as a participation in the mercy of her crucified Son. Francis also recognizes that Mary witnessed her divine Son's words of forgiveness spoken from the Cross: "Father, forgive them, they know not what they do" (Lk 23:34):

> At the foot of the Cross, Mary, together with John, the disciple of love, witnessed the words of forgiveness spoken by Jesus. This supreme expression of mercy toward those who crucified him show us the point to which the mercy of God can reach. Mary attests that the mercy of the Son of God knows no bounds and extends to everyone, without exception. Let us address her in the words of the *Salve Regina*, a prayer ever ancient and ever new, so that she may never tire of turning her merciful eyes upon us, and make us worthy to contemplate the face of mercy, her Son Jesus. (*MV*, 24)

As Mother of Mercy, Mary comes to relieve suffering as she told Mariette at Banneux. She comes asking us to pray so we might receive the merciful forgiveness of her all-merciful Son. By our prayers, we also become instruments of God's mercy—in communion with Christ and our Mother of Mercy.

◇◇

Prayer to Our Lady of Banneux ⚜

O Virgin of the Poor,
May you ever be blessed! And blessed be he who deigned to send you to us.

What you have been and are to us now, you will always be to those who, like us, and better than us, offer their faith and their prayer.

You will be for all of us what you revealed yourself to be at Banneux: Mediatrix of all graces, the Mother of the Savior, Mother of God, a compassionate and powerful mother who loves the poor and all people, who alleviates suffering, who saves individuals and all humanity.

Queen and Mother of all Nations, lead us all to Jesus, the true and only Source of eternal life. Amen.[20]

CHAPTER 9

Mary as Mother of the Church: Our Lady of Fatima

O my Jesus, pardon us, save us from the fires of hell.
Lead all souls to heaven, especially those most in need.
Rosary prayer of OUR LADY OF FATIMA

In our time, where young people often become objects
of exploitation and commerce, these young people excel
as witnesses of truth and freedom, messengers of peace
(and) of a new humanity reconciled in love.
CARDINAL ANGELO AMATO
Canonization of Jacinta and Francisco Marto[1]

On May 13, 2017, Pope Francis solemnly canonized Francisco and Jacinta Marto at a Mass marking the one hundredth anniversary of the first apparition at Fatima, Portugal. The cause of the third visionary, Lucia dos Santos, was opened on April 30, 2008, just three years after her death. Sr. Lucia was present for the beatification of her cousins in 2000, and in 2005, she was laid to rest with them at the Basilica of Our Lady of the Rosary at Fatima. However, Sr. Lucia's canonization process has taken longer because, unlike her cousins who died in childhood, she was "a woman who lived almost ninety-eight years, who corresponded with popes, from Pius VII to John Paul II," amassing a written record of ten thousand letters plus her diary and other written texts.[2]

Her prolific writings can be attributed in part to the three "secrets" that Our Lady gave to the children when she appeared to them six times between May and October 1917. In the apparitions and secrets of Fatima we see the unmistakable image of Mary as Mother of the Church, continually warning, admonishing, and encouraging her children to follow her Son, and to purify themselves with penance, prayer, and continual conversion, fending off the attacks of the enemy not just from outside the Church but also from her faithless children within. Our Lady of the Rosary, Queen of the Church, pray for us.

Fatima, Portugal, 1917

In a small town near Fatima, in the Cova da Iria area of Portugal, three shepherd children reported seeing the Mother of God on May 13, 1917. In addition, they said that an "Angel of Peace" had appeared three times in 1916, and that Mary returned to visit them on the thirteenth of each of the next five months.

According to the children—Lucia dos Santos (ten) and her two younger cousins Francisco Marto (nine) and his sister Jacinta Marto (seven)—the woman was dressed all in white, "more brilliant than the sun dispensing light, clearer and more intense than a crystal cup full of crystalline water penetrated by the rays of the most glaring sun."[3]

On July 13, 1917, on her third appearance to the children, the woman identified herself as Our Lady of the Rosary, and asked the children to pray the Rosary daily for the conversion of sinners. She asked for prayer, penance, and the consecration of Russia to her Immaculate Heart. "In the end my Immaculate Heart will triumph," she said.[4]

The most spectacular of the apparitions was the sixth and final one, which occurred on October 13, 1917, when the Virgin appeared to the children accompanied by St. Joseph and the Christ Child. A crowd of as many as seventy thousand people had gathered in hopes of seeing a sign, and they witnessed perhaps the greatest modern miracle when they saw the sun dance and descend on them, drying their rain-soaked clothes and the land. The "Miracle of the Sun" was witnessed by a crowd of believers and skeptics with people off-site, some as far as forty miles away, reporting seeing the sun dance, spin, and display various colors.

The two younger children did not live long beyond the apparition events. Francisco requested his First Communion on his deathbed and passed away the following day, April 4, 1919. Jacinta Marto died a year later, on February 20, 1920, at the age of nine after an unsuccessful operation for an abscess in her chest.

In June of 1921, the bishop arranged for Lucia to attend a school that was run by the Sisters of St. Dorothy at Pontevedra, Spain; in 1925, she entered their convent in Tui, Spain. Although her sisters were unaware of Lucia's identity, the messages continued. On December 10, 1925, the Virgin Mary introduced the Five First Saturdays devotion to Sr. Lucia:

> See, my daughter, my Heart encircled by thorns with which ungrateful men pierce it at every moment by their blasphemies and ingratitude. Do you, at least, strive to console me? Tell them that I promise to assist at the hour of death with the graces necessary for salvation all those who, in order to make reparation to me, on the First Saturday of five successive months, go to confession, receive Holy Communion, say five decades of the Rosary, and keep me company for a quarter of an hour, meditating on the . . . mysteries of the Rosary.[5]

Recognition by the Church

On October 13, 1930, Dom José Alves Correia da Silva, bishop
of the Diocese of Leiria-Fatima, announced the results of the
investigative commission into the apparitions and formally
approved them as authentic. Pope John Paul II beatified the
two deceased seers, Jacinta and Francisco, on May 13, 2000, and
ordered the feast day of Our Lady of Fatima be made universal,
including it in the Roman Missal.

Canonized on May 13, 2017, they became the youngest
non-martyred saints in the history of the Catholic Church. In
2008, Pope Benedict XVI lifted the normal five-year waiting
period to begin the canonization process of Sr. Lucia dos Santos, who died at age ninety-seven in 2005.

Fatima has become an important place of pilgrimage with
five million people per year coming to the Basilica of Our Lady
of the Rosary,[6] which was begun in 1928 and later consecrated
by Cardinal Cerejeira, the patriarch of Lisbon, in 1956. The
miraculous nature of the events at Fatima has been recognized
by every pope since Pope Pius XII, including Pope Francis, who
dedicated his papacy to Our Lady of Fatima.[7]

Secrets of Fatima

Over the course of the six-month period when she appeared
to the children, the Blessed Virgin gave the children a secret in
three parts (often referred to as the "three secrets").

As recorded in Sr. Lucia's memoir, the first was a terri-
fying vision of hell. In the second part, Our Lady spoke of a
war that would break out during the pontificate of Pius XI.[8]
Our Lady said, "If my requests are heeded, Russia will be converted, and there will be peace; if not, she will spread her errors
throughout the world, causing wars and persecutions of the
Church. The good will be martyred; the Holy Father will have
much to suffer; various nations will be annihilated. . . . In the
end, my Immaculate Heart will triumph. The Holy Father will

consecrate Russia to me, and she shall be converted, and a period of peace will be granted to the world."[9]

On May 13, 2000, Pope John Paul II revealed the third part of the secret with Sr. Lucia in attendance and related the image of a "bishop in white" getting shot. After the assassination attempt by Mehmet Ali Ağca of Turkey in St. Peter's Square on May 13, 1981 (the feast of Our Lady of Fatima), the pope believed that the secret applied to that event. He took the bullet that had entered his body and had it placed in the crown of the famed statue of Our Lady of Fatima in Portugal. Sr. Lucia herself indicated that she agreed with the interpretation of the pope, saying that it was a prophetic vision of the struggle of atheistic communism against Christianity and describes the sufferings of the victims of the faith in the twentieth century.

For the past one hundred years, Our Lady of Fatima has continued to have profound influence on the faithful around the world, as seen by the constant stream of millions of pilgrims yearly and the full acceptance of the events and the revelation of its "secrets" to ecclesial authorities. The messages contained in these secrets as well as the establishment of this Marian feast day on the General Roman Calendar, the construction of a basilica, the canonization of the shepherd children, and visits and official prayers of popes—all these things attest to the fact that Our Lady of Fatima can truly be honored as the Mother of the Church.

The Fatima apparitions are cause for great joy and celebration as are any of the very rare, highly approved, and celebrated examples of the miraculous found in our Church, such as Lourdes, Guadalupe, Divine Mercy, and the Sacred Heart of Jesus visions of St. Margaret Mary Alocoque—examples with papal recognition, canonized visionaries, basilicas, and feast days on the Roman calendar. Whatever the significance of the Fatima apparitions is for each of us personally, we must be reminded of their central message connected with the essence of the message of the gospels: that is, calling us to conversion and bringing us closer to Christ.

Mary as "Mother of the Church" in Scripture and throughout Church History

by Dr. Robert Fastiggi

The 1917 apparitions given to the three shepherd children at Fatima manifest the Blessed Mother's deep concern for the welfare of the Church. As Mother of the Church, Our Lady of Fatima warns the faithful of the dangers of error and hell, and she shows a special concern for the Holy Father, the pope. Her solicitude for the pope is most evident in the three-part secret revealed on July 13, 1917. The first part of the secret is the vision of hell. The second part expands on the purpose of this horrifying vision:

> You have seen hell where the souls of poor sinners go. To save them, God wishes to establish in the world devotion to my Immaculate Heart. If what I say to you is done, many souls will be saved and there will be peace. The war is going to end: but if people do not cease offending God, a worse one will break out during the Pontificate of Pius XI. . . . To prevent this, I shall come to ask for the consecration of Russia to my Immaculate Heart and the Communion of reparation on the First Saturdays. If my requests are heeded, Russia will be converted, and there will be peace; if not, she will spread her errors throughout the world, causing wars and persecutions of the Church. The good will be martyred; the Holy Father will have much to suffer; various nations will be annihilated. In the end, my Immaculate Heart will triumph. The Holy Father will consecrate Russia to me,

and she shall be converted, and a period of peace will be granted to the world.[10]

This second part of the secret shows the concern the Blessed Mother has for the Church and for the pope. She tells the children that "the Holy Father will have much to suffer" and there will be persecutions of the Church. In the end, though, her Immaculate Heart will triumph.

The same concerns of Our Lady of Fatima are evident in the third part of the secret, which was written down by Sr. Lucia on January 3, 1944, but not made known until May 13, 2000, during Pope John Paul II's visit to Fatima to beatify Jacinta and Francisco, two of the seers of Fatima. In the third part of the secret, there is a vision of coming persecutions of the Church:

After the two parts which I have already explained, at the left of Our Lady and a little above, we saw an Angel with a flaming sword in his left hand; flashing, it gave out flames that looked as though they would set the world on fire; but they died out in contact with the splendor that Our Lady radiated towards him from her right hand: pointing to the earth with his right hand, the Angel cried out in a loud voice: "Penance, Penance, Penance!" And we saw in an immense light that is God: "something similar to how people appear in a mirror when they pass in front of it," a Bishop dressed in White; "we had the impression that it was the Holy Father." Other Bishops, Priests, men and women Religious going up a steep mountain, at the top of which there was a big Cross of rough-hewn trunks as of a cork-tree with the bark; before reaching there the Holy Father passed through a big city half in ruins and half trembling with halting step, afflicted with pain and sorrow, he prayed for the souls of the corpses he met on his way; having reached the top of the mountain, on his knees at the foot of the big Cross he was killed by a group of soldiers who fired bullets and arrows at him, and in the same way there died one after another the other Bishops, Priests, men and women Religious, and various lay people of different ranks and positions. Beneath the two arms of the Cross there were two Angels each with a crystal aspersorium in his hand, in which they gathered up the blood of the Martyrs and with it sprinkled the souls that were making their way to God.[11]

In this vision we can see the deep concern of Our Lady for the Holy Father as well as "the Bishops, Priests, men and women Religious, and various lay people of different ranks and positions" who face persecution. Mary, as Mother of the Church, reveals to the three shepherd children that the Church will undergo suffering and martyrdom, but, as a loving mother, she comes to console the Church that the blood of the martyrs will serve as an offering to God.

Why did Mary as Mother of the Church specifically reveal herself as Our Lady of the Rosary?

As Our Lady of the Rosary, Our Lady of Fatima also reveals herself as the Mother of the Church by her maternal charity, as she "cares for the brethren of her Son, who still journey on earth surrounded by dangers and difficulties" (*LG*, 62). The recitation of the Rosary, in fact, highlights Mary as the Mother of the Church. The *Catechism of the Catholic Church* teaches us that "Mary is the perfect *Orans* (prayer), a figure of the Church. When we pray to her, we are adhering with her to the plan of the Father, who sends his Son to save all men. Like the beloved disciple we welcome Jesus' mother into our homes, for she has become the mother of all the living. We can pray with and to her. The prayer of the Church is sustained by the prayer of Mary and united with it in hope" (*CCC*, 2679).

When the memorial of Mary as Mother of the Church was promulgated in February 2018, Cardinal Robert Sarah, the prefect of the Congregation for Divine Worship and the Discipline of the Sacraments, pointed to the Gospel of John as affirming Mary as Mother of the Church: "The Mother standing beneath the cross (cf. Jn 19:25) accepted her Son's testament of love and welcomed all people in the person of the beloved disciple as sons and daughters to be reborn unto life eternal. She thus became the tender Mother of the Church which Christ begot on the cross handing on the Spirit."[12]

Does the title "Mother of the Church" have a scriptural basis?

Mary as Mother of the Church has a long history and deep biblical roots. In John 19:25–27, Mary stands under the Cross of her dying Son, and she is given to the beloved disciple as his own mother. The beloved disciple represents all of the faithful who are to take Mary into their homes. St. John Paul II explains that the Greek for "into his home" (*eis ta idia*) has an even deeper meaning: "Clearly, in the Greek text the expression *'eis ta idia'* goes beyond the mere acceptance of Mary by the disciple in the sense of material lodging and hospitality in his house; it indicates rather a communion of life established between the two as a result of the words of the dying Christ: 'He took her to himself, not into his own property, for he possessed nothing of his own, but among his own duties, which he attended to with dedication'" (*RM*, 130).

John Paul II sees John 19:25–27 as a witness to her labor pains in giving birth to the Church: "Mary united herself to the sacrifice of her Son and made her own maternal contribution to the work of salvation, which took the form of labor pains, the birth of the new humanity."[13]

Furthermore, John Paul II sees this same passage expressing the Marian dimension of the life of every Christian. When we entrust ourselves to Mary in a filial manner, we—like the beloved disciple, John—welcome her into our inner life. The Christian, therefore, "seeks to be taken into that 'maternal charity' with which the Redeemer's Mother 'cares for the brethren of her Son,' 'in whose birth and development she cooperates'

in the measure of the gift proper to each one through the power
of Christ's Spirit" (*RM*, 45).

Where else is "Mother of the Church" found in scripture and tradition?

There are other scriptures that show Mary as the Mother of
the Church. The Blessed Mother is the New Eve (see Genesis
3:15) and the Mother of the Living (see Genesis 3:20), especially
those who have received the new life offered by her divine Son.
Mary, as the Mother of the Church, joins the apostles in prayer
before the coming of the Holy Spirit at Pentecost (see Acts 1:14).
She is also the woman clothed with the sun in Revelation 12:1,
who gives birth to a son "destined to rule all the nations with
an iron rod" (Rv 12:5).[14] The great dragon, the devil, is angry
with her and goes off "to wage war against the rest of her off-
spring" (Rv 12:17).

In addition to these scriptures, there are also the Pauline
references to the Church as the Body of Christ. As Mother of
the Incarnate Word, Mary is the mother of all the faithful who
are joined to the Mystical Body of Christ, which is the Church
(see Romans 12:5; 1 Corinthians 10:16–17, 12:12–31; Ephesians
1:22–23, 5:23–30; and Colossians 1:18–24).

Mary as Mother of the Church finds support from the
Fathers of the Church. St. Augustine (354–430) sees Mary as
"the mother of the members of Christ . . . having cooperated
by charity so the faithful might be born in the Church, who are
members of that Head" (*LG*, 53).

In the Middle Ages, St. Anselm (1033–1109) speaks of Mary
as "the Mother of justification and the justified; the Mother of
reconciliation and the reconciled; the Mother of salvation and of
the saved."[15] Berengaud in the twelfth century explicitly refers
to Mary as "Mother of the Church" (*Mater Ecclesiae*) "because
she brought forth him who is the head of the Church."[16] St.
Bonaventure (ca. 1221–1274) likewise says that the Church took
her origin from Mary.[17] The title of Mary, Mother of the Church,

is found in an Irish litany around the fourteenth century and is used by numerous Catholic writers such as Denis the Carthusian (1402–1471), St. Peter Canisius (1521–1597), and Jean-Jacques Olier (1608–1657).[18]

Many popes have also called Mary Mother of the Church. Pope Benedict XIV, in the papal bull *Gloriosae Dominae* (1748), states that Mary on Calvary is "in the proper sense Mother of the Church, a gift the Church received from the lips of her dying Bridegroom." In more recent times, Pope Leo XIII, in the encyclical *Adiutricem* (1895), extols Mary as "the Mother of the Church, the Teacher and Queen of the Apostles."[19]

After Pope Leo XIII, popes have referred to Mary as Mother of the Church explicitly or in equivalent terms. In his December 4, 1963, address at the close of the Second Session of Vatican II, Pope Paul VI expressed hope that Mary would be honored with the title "Mother of the Church" in the Dogmatic Constitution of the Church.[20] Moreover, Mary, as Mother of the Church, is expressed in equivalent terms in the document: "The Catholic Church, taught by the Holy Spirit, honors [Mary] with filial affection and piety as a most beloved mother."[21]

In response to various requests, Paul VI, in his address at the conclusion of the Third Session of the Second Vatican Council (November 21, 1964), declared the Blessed Virgin Mary to be "Mother of the Church, that is to say of all Christian people, the faithful as well as the pastors, who call her the most loving Mother." He also established that "the Mother of God should be further honored and invoked by the entire Christian people by this title."[22] Paul VI explained that as soon as Christ took on a human nature in Mary's virginal womb, he united to himself, as its head, his Mystical Body, which is the Church. Therefore, "Mary, as the Mother of Christ, must be regarded as the Mother of all the faithful and pastors, which means the Church."[23]

In light of Paul VI's 1964 declaration, a votive Mass in honor of "Blessed Mary Mother of the Church" (*Beata Maria Ecclesiæ Matre*) was proposed during the 1975 Jubilee Year of Reconciliation, and it was later included in the Roman Missal.

In 1980, the Marian title "Mother of the Church" was added to the Litany of Loreto with papal approval. The 1986 *Collection of Masses of the Blessed Virgin Mary* includes three formularies for the celebration of "the Blessed Virgin Mary, Image and Mother of the Church."[24]

What is the significance of the new memorial announced by the Vatican in 2018?

In the decree of February 11, 2018, Cardinal Robert Sarah, prefect of the Congregation for Divine Worship and the Discipline of the Sacraments, announced that "Pope Francis has decreed that the Memorial of the Blessed Virgin Mary, Mother of the Church, should be inscribed in the Roman calendar on the Monday after Pentecost and be celebrated every year."[25] Therefore, in the Latin-rite Church, the celebration of the Blessed Virgin Mary, Mother of the Church, as an obligatory memorial, will have precedence over any other memorial on the Monday following Pentecost.

Pope Francis believes this new obligatory memorial will highlight "the mystery of Mary's spiritual motherhood, which from the awaiting of the Spirit at Pentecost has never ceased to take motherly care of the pilgrim Church on earth," according to Cardinal Sarah. The pope also hopes that the memorial will help us root our spiritual lives "firmly on three great realities: the Cross, the Eucharist, and the Mother of God."[26]

The memorial of Mary as Mother of the Church on the Monday after Pentecost will help us all realize how important Mary, the mystical spouse of the Holy Spirit, is to our lives as Christians. She is truly our mother "in the order of grace" (*LG*, 61). She is united to Christ, the Head of the Church, "by a close and indissoluble" bond (*LG*, 53), and she is united to us as our spiritual mother, the Mother of the Church.

At Fatima, Mary revealed herself as the Mother of the Church in a powerful way. She warned the children of the sufferings the Holy Father and the faithful would face in the future. She consoled them with the assurance that in the end, her Immaculate Heart will triumph.

◇◇◇

PRAYER TO OUR LADY OF FATIMA ⚜

Hail, Mother of the Lord, Virgin Mary, Queen of the Rosary of Fatima!
Blessed among all women, you are the image of the Church robed in paschal light, you are the honor of our people, you are the victory over every assault of evil.

Prophecy of the merciful love of the Father,

Teacher of the message of Good News of the Son,

Sign of the burning fire of the Holy Spirit, teach us, in this valley of joys and sorrows, the eternal truths that the Father reveals to the little ones.

Show us the strength of your protective mantle.

In your Immaculate Heart, be the refuge of sinners and the way that leads to God.

In union with my brothers and sisters, in faith, in hope, and in love, I entrust myself to you.

In union with my brothers and sisters, through you, I consecrate myself to God, O Virgin of the Rosary of Fatima.

And at last, enveloped in the Light that comes from your hands, I will give glory to the Lord for ever and ever. Amen.[27]

CHAPTER 10

Mary as Queen of Heaven: Our Lady of Beauraing

The important part that Mary plays in our salvation is not well enough understood. Many Catholics look upon devotion to Our Lady as something that has been added to the Christian life. They look upon it as an accessory . . . one that we could, strictly speaking, do without. The truth is that we depend upon Mary for our supernatural life just as a child depends on his earthly mother for his natural life. St. Louis de Montfort said that "all the predestinate . . . are hidden in the womb of the most holy Virgin, where they are guarded, nourished, and made to grow by that good Mother until she has brought them forth to glory after death."

BISHOP ANDRE-MARIE CHARUE OF NAMUR
July 2, 1949[1]

I am the Mother of God, the Queen of Heaven. Pray always. Goodbye.

OUR LADY OF BEAURAING to Andrée Degeimbre
January 2, 1933

The apparitions of Banneux and Beauraing are very similar, separated by a few days and about fifty miles. Why would Mary make two appearances so close together in both time and space? Could it be that, from the vantage of heaven, she could see the destruction that would soon be unleashed by the forces of Hitler across the continent? It's possible.

What we do know is that, as with all Marian devotional titles, Mary's queenship is closely tied to her motherhood. The appearance of Mary at Beauraing, just a few days prior to her appearance as "Virgin of the Poor" at Banneux, reveals her heart of gold that beats with love for all her children. In the letter to the clergy, the local bishop stated, "We are able in all serenity and prudence to affirm that the Queen of Heaven appeared to the children of Beauraing during the winter of 1932–1933, especially to show us in her maternal Heart the anxious appeal for prayer and the promise of her powerful mediation for the conversion of sinners."[2] In the Lady of the Golden Heart we are reminded that, like any good mother, Mary remains close to her children when they are most in need of her.

Beauraing, Belgium, 1932–1933

Throughout Christian history, the Virgin Mary has been said to appear to people from all walks of life in places all around the world. When the data on her appearances are examined, she appears most commonly to young people in Europe. The story of the visions of Beauraing fits that mold.

She appeared on a playground of a convent school to five children who belonged to two families: the Voisin children: Fernande (fifteen), Gilberte (thirteen), and Albert (eleven); and the Degeimbre girls: Andrée (fourteen) and Gilberte (nine). These were working families of nonpracticing Catholics.

It was reported that between November 29, 1932, and January 3, 1933, the Mother of God had appeared thirty-three times. During the last apparition on January 3, 1933, she asked for prayers for the conversion of sinners and identified herself as the "Queen of Heaven."

The Visions

November 29, 1932, started as a normal day, as the children did as they almost always would do: Albert and Fernande Voisin and Andrée and Gilberte Degeimbre approached the door of a convent school run by the Sisters of Christian Doctrine to call for Gilberte Voisin. On this occasion, Albert ran ahead of the girls and rang the bell on the convent door.

As he awaited an answer at the door, he gazed toward the street and bridge for the railroad and saw a figure illuminated. He yelled to the others: "Look! The Virgin, dressed in white, is walking above the bridge!" Turning around, the girls saw the beautiful white-clad figure of a woman carrying a rosary with clouds obscuring her feet and walking above the bridge and the convent's grotto.

When she came to the door, Gilberte Voisin saw the vision, but the religious sister who accompanied her could not see the figure. Albert asked the vision, "Are you the Immaculate Virgin?" She responded with a smile and a nod. When he asked further, "What do you want?" she responded with the exhortation for the children to "always be good."[3]

The Messages

In the thirty-three visions at Beauraing, the Virgin Mary urged the children to pray and sacrifice, asking "that people pray much." During the fourth apparition (December 4) and the seventh (December 21), the Virgin clearly stated, "I am the Immaculate Virgin."[4]

On December 17, she had requested that a chapel be built there. When she appeared again on December 23, the children asked her the reason she was appearing to them. She answered, "That people might come here on pilgrimage." When the Virgin extended her arms in farewell on December 29, she revealed an illuminated and glittering heart of gold surrounded by rays of light that all the children continued to witness during the final five visits, as she admonished them to "pray, pray a lot!"[5]

The Virgin Mary appeared for the final time with twenty thousand faithful gathered at Beauraing on January 3, 1933. She left them with a promise very similar to the one she made at Lourdes: "I will convert sinners," adding, "I am the Mother of God, the Queen of Heaven."[6]

Church Approval

As is typical in most apparition accounts, the children's parents did not believe them. Nor did the mother superior of the convent where the children had seen the visions believe them; Mother Theophile encouraged them to stop talking about the alleged sighting.

The bishop of Namur, Thomas Louis-Heylen, appointed an episcopal commission to investigate the events. An examination of the occurrences was initiated. The tests were very similar to those done on St. Bernadette Soubirous at Lourdes while she experienced her visions. During the December 8 apparition at Beauraing, Dr. Maistriaux, Dr. Lurquin, and other doctors performed stimulus tests to pinch, slap, and prick the children and shine flashlights in their eyes. There was no response from the children during the apparition. Dr. Lurquin put Gilberte Voisin's left hand in a flame, but there was no physical reaction or sign of injury.[7]

When the bishop died in 1941, the investigation continued under his successor, Bishop Andre-Marie Charue.[8] After long investigations and consultation of the primate of Belgium, Cardinal Van Roy, with Rome, the cult of Our Lady of Beauraing was recognized by Bishop Charue on February 2, 1943. He then released a document on July 2, 1949, to clergy in the diocese declaring that the Queen of Heaven had appeared to the children. Additionally, a positive ruling was given on "the miraculous nature of two cures obtained through the intercession of Our Lady of Beauraing."[9] Construction of the chapel was begun in 1947, and it was consecrated on August 21, 1954, bringing to a close the fulfillment of the request of the Virgin Mary "that a chapel be built."

The feast day of the Virgin of the Poor is August 22, and the statue of Our Lady of Beauraing was blessed and canonically crowned on August 22, 1946, on the feast of the Immaculate Heart, later to be called the Queenship of the Blessed Virgin Mary. Pope John Paul II visited Beauraing on May 18, 1985, which in itself is a sign of Vatican recognition for a miraculous event.

As is typically the case with approved apparitions, most notably at Lourdes, there is often aping of the authentic events by others purporting to experience similar phenomena. This was definitely the case in Belgium where back-to-back approved Marian apparitions in Banneux and Beauraing spawned false claims that multiplied throughout the country in places such as Onkerzele, Lokeren, Naastveld, Tubize, Olsene, and Etikhove.

The visionaries went on to live normal, quiet lives. All five children eventually married and had at least two children of their own. Fernande moved with her family to Namur; Andrée remained with her family in Beauraing; and Albert, Gilberte Voisin, and Gilberte Degeimbre all returned to Beauraing after having moved away for some time.

On June 11, 1978, Andrée Degeimbre was the first of the five to pass away, followed by Fernande Voisin in 1979 and Albert Voisin in 2003. Gilberte Voison had a fatal accident on January 3, 2003, the seventieth anniversary of the last apparition, at the exact hour that the Virgin Mary said, "I will convert sinners." The last living visionary, Gilberte Degeimbre, died on February 10, 2015, at the age of ninety-one.

Mary as "Queen of Heaven" in Scripture and throughout Church History

by Dr. Robert Fastiggi

On January 3, 1933, Mary made her final appearance to the children at Beauraing. On that day, she told Andrée: "I am the Mother of God, the Queen of Heaven. Pray always."[10]

Mary has long been recognized by the Church in exceptional terms and with great reverence and honor. In the fifth Glorious Mystery, we meditate on Mary's coronation, on her distinction as Queen of Heaven and Earth. This title is again preserved and recalled each year on August 22, the Feast of the Queenship of Mary. It is indisputable that the Church wishes to honor Mary for her divine motherhood as well as for her role in God's plan of salvation for all people.

What does the Bible say about Mary's queenship?

Mary's queenship is prefigured in the Old Testament. The queen mother (or *gebirah*, "great lady") is present in 1 Kings 2:19 as Bathsheba, King Solomon's mother. When Bathsheba goes to King Solomon to intercede on behalf of Adonijah, the king rises to meet her, and he pays her homage. He provides a throne for his mother, and she sits on his right. When his mother reveals she has a favor to ask of him, the king immediately replies: "Ask it, my mother, for I will not refuse you" (1 Kgs 2:20). As Scott Hahn notes, even though Solomon technically was his mother's superior, "in the orders of both nature and protocol he remained her son."[11]

The queen mother played a crucial role in the running of the kingdom, for while a king at that time could have many wives, he had only one mother. She was responsible for selecting his heir (often but not always the eldest son) and would also serve as a "sounding board" for those who wanted the king's attention.

When the angel appears to Mary and announces that she is about to become the mother of the Messiah, he says to her, "He will be great and will be called Son of the Most High, and the Lord God will give him the throne of David his father, and he will rule over the house of Jacob forever, and of his kingdom there will be no end" (Lk 1:32–33). The significance of this pronouncement would have been clear: Mary was to be the mother of a king—that is, the queen mother!

Although Mary is a queen, she always uses her royal status in service toward others. At the wedding feast of Cana (see John 2:1–11), Mary shows herself to be the queen-advocate who demonstrates her "compassion and attentiveness to others' needs."[12] Her royal dignity is expressed by acting, in the words of Pope John Paul II, "as a mediatrix . . . in her position as mother."[13]

The New Testament also presents Mary as the woman of Revelation 12:1, who wears a crown of twelve stars. As Edward Sri explains, "In the book of Revelation the symbol of the crown is never a superfluous decoration, but denotes a real reign."[14]

Has Mary's queenship been recognized in Catholic history?

There is continuous testimony to Mary's queenship from the patristic age to the present. Origen (ca. 185–254) called Mary "Lady" (*kuria*), which is the feminine of *kyrios* or "Lord."[15] This is because Elizabeth greets Mary as the "Mother of my Lord" (Lk 1:43). St. Ephrem of Syria (ca. 306–373) spoke of Mary as "Majestic and Heavenly Maid, Lady, Queen."[16] St. Andrew of Crete (ca. 660–740) extolled the Blessed Mother as "the Queen of the human race,"[17] and St. John Damascene (ca. 674–750) praised Mary as "the Queen of every creature."[18]

During the Middle Ages, Mary's queenship was recognized by writers such as Peter Damian, Anselm, Eadmerus, and Bernard of Clairvaux.[19] The great Marian hymns of the medieval period—such as the *Salve Regina, Ave Regina Caelorum,* and the *Regina Caeli* as well as the Litany of Loreto—all invoked the Blessed Mother as queen.[20] The fifth decade of the Glorious Mysteries of the Rosary continues to pay homage to Mary's coronation as Queen of Heaven and of Earth. Catholic art of the Middle Ages frequently depicted Mary as a queen "seated on a throne . . . wearing royal clothes, surrounded by angels and saints venerating her, and even being crowned by her Son."[21]

The recognition of Mary's queenship continued into the early modern era. Catholic authors such as Francisco Suárez (1548–1617), St. Louis de Montfort (1673–1716), and St. Alphonsus Liguori (1696–1787) honored Mary as queen and provided reasons for her royal dignity.

Is there Magisterial support for Mary as queen?

There has indeed been much support from the Magisterium for Mary's queenship. Pope Gregory II wrote a letter to the patriarch Germanus calling Mary "the Queen of all" and "the Queen of all Christians."[22] This letter was read at the Second Council of Nicaea in 787 "with all the Fathers concurring."[23] In his 1477 constitution on the Immaculate Conception, Pope Sixtus IV extolled Mary as "the Queen of heaven,"[24] and Benedict XIV, in his 1748 papal bull, *Gloriosae Dominae,* referred to the Blessed Mother as "Queen of heaven and earth" to whom "the Sovereign King has in some way communicated . . . his ruling power."[25] The popes from Leo XIII up to the present have spoken of Mary by such titles as "Queen of Peace," "Queen of the Apostles," and "Queen of the Martyrs."[26]

The most complete exposition of Mary's queenship is the October 11, 1954, encyclical of Pope Pius XII titled *Ad Caeli Reginam,* which established the Feast of the Queenship of Mary. In this encyclical, the Holy Father provides an overview of the scriptural, patristic, and liturgical supports for Mary's queenship. He states that the "main principle on which the royal dignity of Mary rests is without doubt her Divine Motherhood."[27] He also notes that "the Virgin Mary should be called Queen, not only because of her Divine Motherhood, but also because God has willed her to have an exceptional role in the work of our eternal salvation."[28] Quoting the great Jesuit theologian Suárez, Pius XII notes that just as Christ "is our Lord and king by a special title, so the Blessed Virgin also [is our queen] on account of the unique manner in which she assisted in our redemption, by giving of her own substance, by freely offering Him for us, by her singular desire and petition for, and active interest in, our salvation."[29]

Pius XII originally established May 31 as the Feast of the Queenship of Mary. After Vatican II, the feast was moved to August 22 so that it would follow within the octave of the Solemnity of the Assumption. The Vatican II refers to Mary as "the Queen of the universe" in *Lumen Gentium* (59). As our heavenly queen, Mary is our spiritual mother who never ceases to intercede for us before the throne of her divine Son. May we always honor her as our mother and our queen, especially the queen of our hearts.

◇◇

PRAYER TO OUR LADY OF BEAURAING ⚜

Our Lady of Beauraing, Immaculate Virgin, Carry to Jesus, your Son, all the intentions which we confide to you this day.
(Here mention your intentions)

Mother with the Golden Heart, mirror of the tenderness of the Father, look with love upon the men and women of our time and fill them with the joy of your presence.

You who promised to convert sinners, help us to discover the infinite mercy of our God. Awaken in us the grace of conversion so that all our life becomes the reflection of this mercy.

Holy Mother of God, look down upon our miseries, console us in our sorrows, give strength to all those who are suffering.

Queen of Heaven, crowned with light, help us grow in faith, hope, and love, and we shall be able to give thanks without end.

You brought Jesus into the world. Pray for us, that in word and deed we might share the love and joy of the One who is born in our hearts. May every instant of our lives be a positive affirmation of the two questions you are asking of us, even now: *Do you love my Son? Do you love me?*

When at last we can say *yes* with all our hearts, then the reign of Jesus will come into the world. Amen.[30]

CONCLUSION

Mary in Most Recent Times: What Is She Saying Today?

by Michael O'Neill

Reports of Marian apparitions and devotion to the Mother of God date back to the beginnings of Christianity and continue in our world today. Pilgrims can still travel to Zaragoza, Spain, and kiss the pillar that, according to pious tradition, was the one on which the Virgin Mary appeared to St. James in the year 40. (See image at left.) Although she was still living at the time, it is considered the earliest known vision of the Mother of God.

According to later accounts of the miracle, St. James was despairing and struggling to gain traction in preaching the Gospel in Spain. Then one day near the Ebro River, the Virgin Mary bilocated to be with him, encouraging him while standing on a pillar of jasper. The common Spanish girl's name *Pilar* is reminiscent of this early Marian miracle story.

As history has marched on, there have been countless other claims of the Virgin Mary interceding on our behalf, only a scant few of which are ever investigated by an episcopal commission or officially approved by the local bishop. Even fewer have received any sort of Vatican recognition. On very rare occasions, Rome has cemented certain Marian apparitions in the pantheon of believable supernatural events by establishing a feast day in the General Roman Calendar, canonizing the visionary, establishing a basilica, or arranging a papal visit (often accompanied by the bestowing of the treasured Golden Rose or a special prayer invoking that Marian title).

In the most highly approved and celebrated cases of Marian apparitions throughout history, the Virgin Mary has been said typically to appear a small number of times. (The notable exception is that of the 1664 Church-approved visions at Le Laus in France, where shepherdess Benoite Rencurel received visions on one day and then every day of her life afterward.)

Since the turn of the twentieth century, Mary seems to appear with greater frequency at each purported apparition site. As Mother of the Word in Kibeho, Rwanda, she appeared hundreds of times to the schoolchildren. Similarly, frequent visions and messages were reported by Ida Peerdeman (Amsterdam, 1945), by Maria Esperanza (Betania, Venezuela, 1976), by Sr. Agnes Sasagawa (Akita, Japan, 1973), and by Gladys Quiroga de Motta (San Nicolás, Argentina, 1983). These visits and messages have all received approval of their local bishop, though they have yet to receive discernible recognition from the Vatican. (It may simply be a matter of time before they are shown some favor by Rome, but perhaps they will simply stand as having been supported by a single bishop.)

Whereas in an earlier age of approved apparitions the Virgin Mary appeared most commonly to children and teenagers, more modern apparitions have been claimed by visionaries with an older profile, typically in their forties and beyond. Perhaps with the bucking of this established trend of Mary appearing to the young and simple, approvals from the Church in more modern times have become more rare as the newer claims seem to fall outside the pattern.

In more recent times we have also seen the previously rare phenomena of the de-emphasis or even reversal of several previously approved rulings regarding the supernatural character of alleged apparitions, as various factors lead those responsible for discernment to question the authenticity of a particular vision or message.

Deep in the Amazon in Itapiranga, Brazil, for example, the visions of the young man Edson Glauber received some preliminary approvals and indications of the bishop's belief in the supernaturality of the events, but the devotion has since been discouraged (as of 2017). Similarly, in San Nicolás, Argentina, the approval of the apparitions has not received a reversal, but new messages will not be released or examined by the current local bishop. And in Japan, despite the bishop's approval and scientific tests that identified human tears and blood emanating from a wooden statue of the Virgin Mary, the devotion has been tempered.

The 1948 apparitions at Lipa in the Philippines to Carmelite novice Teresita Castillo were judged in 2016 to be authentic by Bishop Ramon C. Arguelles when he reversed the long-standing Vatican prohibition against them. Months later, the Vatican reversed his reversal.

Beyond those cases from the twentieth century that have inspired controversy, in modern times there have been hundreds of other locations with alleged claims. Most have been ignored and others investigated, with some given a "wait-and-see" status, including famous cases at Garabandal in Spain in the 1960s and Medjugorje in Bosnia-Herzegovina in the 1980s and beyond. While some appearances have included dire warnings for their nations, such as at Kibeho, all seem to share the common themes of prayer, penance, and a call to return to Christ.

As we turn to the Church for guidance and use discernment before incorporating any claim of private revelation into our lives of faith, we recognize the Virgin Mary in our hearts as our mother, watching out for us, and we respond faithfully to her invitation to draw closer to her Son. As we ponder Mary's many titles and miraculous intercessions throughout history, we come to know her more deeply and find inspiration in her example.

NOTES

Introduction

1. "Shelter from the Fire," Website of the National Shrine of Our Lady of Good Help (OLGH), https://www.shrineofourladyofgood-help.com/about-our-shrine/. Accessed June 6, 2019.

1. Mary as Blessed

1. "The Official Testimonies of the Fifteen Witnesses to the Knock Apparition on 21 August 1879," Knock Shrine website, http://www.knockshrine.ie/wp-content/uploads/2014/12/Witness-Accounts.pdf. Accessed June 6, 2019.

2. W. J. Smith, *The Mystery of Knock: Our Lady in Ireland* (New York: Paulist Press, 1954), 16.

3. "Official Testimonies," Knock Shrine website.

4. "Official Testimonies," Knock Shrine website.

5. "History—Commissions of Enquiry," Knock Shrine website, http://www.knockshrine.ie/history/commissions-of-enquiry. Accessed June 6, 2019.

6. Donal Foley, *Marian Apparitions, the Bible, and the Modern World* (Herefordshire, England: Gracewing Publishing, 2002), 212.

7. The Golden Rose is a traditional Catholic ornament with origins dating back to the fifteenth century. See "Golden Rose," New Advent, http://www.newadvent.org/cathen/06629a.htm.

8. *New World Dictionary-Concordance to the New American Bible* (New York: C. D. Stampley Enterprises, 1970), 66–67. (Hereafter *NWD-C.*)

9. From the "Divine Praises" in *The Liturgy of the Hours: Evening Prayer*, February 2, 2018 (9). Ebreviary.com.

10. Ephrem the Syrian, *Hymns on the Nativity* 25, 12, as cited in
Luigi Gambero, *Mary and the Fathers of the Church*, trans. Thomas
Buffer (San Francisco: Ignatius Press, 1999), 110.

11. "Prayer to Our Lady of Knock," Knock, Shrine website,
https://www.knockshrine.ie/prayers.

2. Mary as Virgin

1. See Heinrich Denzinger and Peter Hünermann, eds., *Compendium of Creeds, Definitions, and Declarations on Matters of Faith and Morals*, 43rd ed. (San Francisco: Ignatius Press, 2012), 10–30. (thereafter D-H.)

2. See Monsignor Eduardo Chávez, *The Woman Who Changed the Face of a Hemisphere* (Guadalupanos A.R.: Instituto Superior de Estudios Guadalupanos), 9.

3. According to Dr. Timothy Matovina, professor of theology at Notre Dame and author of *Theologies of Guadalupe: From the Era of Conquest to Pope Francis,* support for the position that "Guadalupe" was a mispronunciation of a Nahuatl word can be traced to a seventeenth-century treatise by Luis Becerra Tanco.

4. "Our Lady of Guadalupe," Catholicism.org, June 10, 2004
https://catholicism.org/brmichael-guadalupe.html

5. "Our Lady of Guadalupe 'completely beyond' scientific explanation, says researcher," Catholic News Agency, August 7, 2009,
https://www.catholicnewsagency.com/news/our_lady_of_guadalupe_completely_beyond_scientific_explanation_says_researcher.

6. Philip Serna Callahan, "The Tilma under Infra-Red Radiation, CARA Studies on Popular Devotion," *Guadalupan Studies*, Vol. 2, No. 3 (Washington, DC: Center for Applied Research in the Apostolate, 1981).

7. A fascinating account of the events leading up to this declaration may be found in the January–April 1885 edition of *The Month: A Catholic Magazine and Review* (London: Burns and Oates), 341–342. Available on Google Books.

8. See Timothy Ware, *The Orthodox Church* (London: Penguin Books, 1993), 257–258.

9. See Max Thurian, *Mary: Mother of All Christians* (New York: Herder, 1964), 37–41.

10. See Matthew 12:46–50, 13:55–56, and 28:10; Mark 3:31–35 and 6:3; Luke 8:19–21; John 2:12, 7:3, 5, 10, and 20:17; Acts 1:14; 1

Corinthians 9:5; and Galations 1:19. None of the sisters (*adelphai*) of Jesus are mentioned by name.

11. See François Rossier, S.M., "The 'Brothers and Sisters' of Jesus: Anything New?" in *Marian Studies* 58 (2007): 104–107.

12. The identity of this "other Mary" is not revealed in scripture, though she is not one of the more familiar figures in the gospels, such as Mary Magdalene or Mary of Bethany (the sister of Martha and Lazarus).

13. For example, in Genesis 14:14 and 16, Lot is referred to as Abraham's "brother" (*'ah*) in the King James Version. However, we know from Genesis 11:27 that Lot was the son of Abraham's brother Haran, which would make him Abraham's nephew. When Genesis 14:14 and 16 are translated into Greek in the Septuagint, *'ah* is translated as *adelphos* or "brother." This shows that in biblical Greek, brother (*adelphos*) could mean close relative as well as blood brother. In light of this usage, James and Joseph could be referred to as Jesus' "brothers" even though they are sons of another Mary.

14. See Exodus 4:22–23 and Jeremiah 31:9.

15. Both the Vulgate and the Nova Vulgata versions of scripture use *usque*, which may be translated "until."

16. See Jaroslav Pelikan, *Mary Through the Centuries: Her Place in the History of Culture* (New Haven: Yale University Press, 1996), 29.

17. D-H, 503. The Creed of the Sixth Council of Toledo, AD 638, declares that the Word assumed sinless humanity from the holy ever-virgin Mary (*de sancta semper virgine Maria*) (D-H, 491). At the Lateran Council of 649, those who did not confess that Jesus "was incarnate from the Holy Spirit and the most holy Mary, ever virgin" (*semper virgine*) were anathematized (D-H, 502). Furthermore, those who denied that Mary gave birth to Jesus "without corruption, her virginity remaining equally inviolate after the birth" (*et incorruptibiliter eam genuisse, indissolubii permanente et post partum eisdem virginitate*) were condemned (D-H, 503).

18. Juan Luis Bastero, *Mary, Mother of the Redeemer*, trans. Michael Adams and Philip Griffin (Dublin: Four Courts Press), 174, footnote 41.

19. See *Lumen Gentium*, 57. (*Lumen Gentium* is hereafter abbreviated as *LG*.) The footnote to this passage cites not only the Lateran Synod of 649 but also statements by Pope Leo I, the Council of Chalcedon, and St. Ambrose that make it clear that Mary's physical integrity was preserved.

20. *Acta Apostolicae Sedis* 85 (1993), 665.

21. Gambero, *Mary and the Fathers,* 71; *LG,* 64–65; John Paul II, *Behold Your Mother: Mary in the Life of the Priests* (1988), 5.

22. Gambero, *Mary and the Fathers,* 207.

23. Gambero, *Mary and the Fathers,* 167; the Akathist Hymn: "Hail, thou who didst comprehend the incomprehensible . . . Hail! Bride Unbrided," Gambero, *Mary and the Fathers,* 348; John Paul II, *Mother of the Redeemer,* 43.

24. Gambero, *Mary and the Fathers,* 157, 221; Thomas Aquinas, *Summa Theologica* III, q. 28, a. 4. (Summa Theologica is hereafter abbreviated as *ST.*)

25. Gambero, *Mary and the Fathers,* 191.

26. Gambero, *Mary and the Fathers,* 123.

27. Gambero, *Mary and the Fathers,* 178.

28. Gambero, *Mary and the Fathers,* 207; Thomas Aquinas, *ST* III, q. 28, a. 3.

29. Gambero, *Mary and the Fathers,* 287; Thomas Aquinas, *ST* III, q. 28, a. 3.

30. Gambero, *Mary and the Fathers,* 211.

31. Cf. Thomas Aquinas, *ST* III, q. 28, a. 3.

32. Cf. Thomas Aquinas, *ST* III, q. 28, a. 3.

33. Adapted from "John Paul II's Prayer to Our Lady of Guadalupe," United States Conference of Catholic Bishops website, http://www.usccb.org/issues-and-action/cultural-diversity/hispanic-latino/resources/upload/our-lady-of-guadalupe-jp-II-prayer.pdf. Accessed June 11, 2019.

3. Mary as Mother of God

1. Immaculée Ilibagiza, *Our Lady of Kibeho* (Carlsbad, CA: Hay House, 2008), 40–41.

2. Ilibagiza, *Our Lady of Kibeho,* 148–149.

3. Fr. Ubald Rugirangoga's story is told in the book *Forgiveness Makes You Free: A Dramatic Story of Healing and Reconciliation from the Heart of Rwanda* (Notre Dame, IN: Ave Maria Press, 2019).

4. "Judgment on the Apparitions of Kibeho," EWTN website, https://www.ewtn.com/library/MARY/OLKIBEHO.HTM. Accessed June 11, 2019.

5. Zenit News Agency, "Yes, the Virgin Mary Did Appear in Kibeho," https://zenit.org/articles/yes-the-virgin-mary-did-appear-in-kibeho July 2, 2001. Accessed June 3, 2019.

6. "Judgment on the Apparitions of Kibeho," EWTN website.

7. Joan Carroll Cruz, *See How She Loves Us* (Charlotte, NC: Tan Books, 2012), 230.

8. "Mary: The Most Powerful Woman in the World," in *National Geographic Magazine*, December, 2015 (45).

9. "Judgment on the Apparitions of Kibeho," EWTN website.

10. "Judgment on the Apparitions of Kibeho," EWTN website.

11. "Jubilee Year to Focus on Mary's Message in Rwanda," Zenit News Agency, November 13, 2006. https://zenit.org/articles/jubilee-year-to-focus-on-mary-s-message-in-rwanda. Accessed June 6, 2019.

12. "Kibeho Jubilee," University of Dayton—International Marian Research Institute, https://udayton.edu/imri/mary/k/kibeho-jubilee.php. Accessed June 3, 2019.

13. D-H, 250–251.

14. See Mar Bawai Soro, *The Church of the East: Apostolic & Orthodox* (San Jose, CA: Adiabene Publications, 2007), 233–259.

15. *Common Christological Declaration between the Catholic Church and the Assyrian Church of the East* (November 11, 1994), http://www.vatican.va/roman_curia/pontifical_councils/chrstuni/documents/rc_pc_chrstuni_doc_11111994_assyrian-church_en.html.

16. Michael O'Carroll, C.S.Sp., *Theotokos: A Theological Encyclopedia of the Blessed Virgin Mary* (Eugene, OR: Wipf and Stock, 2000), 94.

17. The Creed of Nicaea-Constantinople in D-H, 150.

18. Anthony M. Buono, *The Greatest Marian Prayers: Their History, Meaning, and Usage* (New York: Alba House, 1999), 36.

19. Gambero, *Mary and the Fathers*, 101.

20. D-H, 301.

21. D-H, 427.

22. D-H, 503.

23. Cf. D-H, 294.

4. Mary as Immaculate and All-Holy

1. Roy Abraham Varghese, *God Sent: A History of the Accredited Apparitions of Mary* (New York: Crossroad Publishing Company, 2000), 104.

2. "Extracts from the Cross Examination of Bernadette Soubirous," Biography Online, https://www.biographyonline.net/spiritual/articles/bernadette-examination.html. Accessed June 11, 2019.

3. This refers to the inexplicable preservation of the mortal remains of a person, which is often seen to be a sign of God's favor and demonstration of holiness.

4. Frances Parkinson Keyes, "Bernadette and the Beautiful Lady," in *A Woman Clothed with the Sun: Eight Great Apparitions of Our Lady,* ed. John J. Delaney (New York: Doubleday Image Books, 1999), 137. (Hereafter, "*Woman Clothed.*")

5. Cf. Pius IX, Bull, *Ineffabilis Deus* (December 8, 1854), in D-H, n. 2800–2804.

6. It should be noted that in the 43rd edition of Denzinger-Hünermann's *Compendium* (English ed., 2012), 2800, the reference to the foreseen wretchedness of the human race is omitted via ellipsis.

7. Leo I, Tome to Flavian, D-H, 293–294.

8. Settimo M. Manelli, F.I., "The Virgin Mary in the New Testament," in *Mariology: A Guide for Priests, Deacons, Seminarians, and Consecrated Persons,* ed. Mark Miravalle (Goleta, CA: Queenship Publishing, 2007), 75.

9. Ephrem the Syrian, *Carmina Nisibena* 28, 8, as cited in Gambero, *Mary and the Fathers,* 109.

10. Andrew of Crete, *Canon on the Nativity,* in J. P. Migne, *Patrologia Graeca* [PG], 162 vols. (Paris, 1857–1866), Vol. 97: 1321 C.

11. Andrew of Crete, *Canon on the Nativity,* in Migne, PG 97: 1309A.

12. Andrew of Crete, *Homily 1 on the Nativity,* PG 87: 809 D–812 A, as cited in Gambero, *Mary and Fathers,* 394.

13. PG 98: 292–309.

14. John of Damascus, *Homily on the Nativity of the Blessed Virgin* 2, PG 96: 664 A, as cited in Gambero, *Mary and Fathers,* 402.

15. Francis Dvornik, "The Byzantine Church and the Immaculate Conception," in *The Dogma of the Immaculate Conception,* ed. E. D. O'Connor, C.S.C. (Notre Dame, IN: University of Notre Dame Press, 1958), 97.

16. Paul Haffner, *The Mystery of Mary* (Herefordshire, England: Gracewing, 2004), 81.

17. Haffner, *Mystery,* 81. The choice of December 9 as the feast of Mary's conception makes sense because it occurs almost nine months prior to the feast of Mary's nativity (September 8). Later, December 8 was thought to be more appropriate in the West.

18. Haffner, *Mystery*, 81–82. See also Frederick Jelly, O.P., *Madonna: Mary in the Catholic Tradition* (Huntington, IN: Our Sunday Visitor, 1986), 110–11.

19. D-H, 539.

20. Thomas Aquinas, *ST* III, q. 27, a. 2. ad. 2, in *St. Thomas Aquinas: Summa Theologica* Volume IV, trans. by the Fathers of the English Dominican Province (Allen, TX: Christian Classics, 1981), 2159.

21. Aquinas, *ST* III, q. 27, a. 2. ad. 2, in *St. Thomas Aquinas*.

22. Aquinas, *ST* III, q. 27, a. 2. ad. 2.

23. Cf. O'Carroll, *Theotokos*, 321.

24. Peter Fehlner, F.I., "The Predestination of the Virgin Mother and Her Immaculate Conception," in Minavalle, *Mariology*, 257–258.

25. Fehlner, "Predestination," in Minavalle, *Mariology*, 258.

26. D-H, 1425–1426.

27. D-H, 1516.

28. D-H, 1973.

29. O'Carroll, *Theotokos*, 181.

30. O'Carroll, *Theotokos*, 2017.

31. O'Carroll, *Theotokos*, 2324.

32. Jelly, *Madonna*, 114.

33. Jelly, *Madonna*, 114; see also the introduction to D-H, 2800–2804.

34. Adapted from "Novena to the Immaculate Conception," Lourdes Sanctuaire website, https://www.lourdes-france.org/en/prayers. Accessed June 3, 2019.

5. Mary as Mother of Sorrows

1. "The Secret of La Salette: Written statement by Melanie Mathieu on July 6, 1851" http://www.miraclehunter.com/marian_apparitions/approved_apparitions/lasalette/secret-of-our-lady-of-lasalette-to-melanie-1851.html

2. Catherine M. Odell, *Those Who Saw Her: Apparitions of Mary* (Huntington, IN: Our Sunday Visitor, 2010), 84.

3. Odell, *Those Who Saw*, 84.

4. John S. Kennedy, "The Lady in Tears," in *Woman Clothed*, 75.

5. Kennedy, "The Lady in Tears," in *Woman Clothed*, 76. Ellipses have been added to account for interrupted text from the book.

6. Kennedy, "The Lady in Tears," in *Woman Clothed*, 75.

7. Kennedy, "The Lady in Tears," in *Woman Clothed*, 76.

8. Mélanie rewrote and resubmitted the secrets several times, the final time being a controversial expanded, more detailed version published on November 15, 1879, with the imprimatur of Bishop Salvatore Luigi Zola; it was later censured by Rome and placed on the Index of Forbidden Books. The secrets of La Salette have never received formal approval from the Vatican.

9. Cruz, *See How She Loves Us*, 110.

10. See Vatican II, *Sacrosanctum Concilium* (1963), 103.

11. O'Carroll, *Theotokos*, 167.

12. O'Carroll, *Theotokos*, 167.

13. Brigid of Sweden, *Revelations*, lib. I, c. 35, cited in Gambero, *Mary and the Fathers*, 277.

14. Brigid of Sweden, *Revelations*, lib. I, c. 35; cited in Gambero, *Mary and the Fathers*, 277.

15. Louis de Montfort, "Letter to Friends of the Cross," n. 31, in *God Alone: The Collected Writings of St. Louis Marie de Montfort* (Bay Shore, NY: Montfort Publications, 1988), 134.

16. O'Carroll, *Theotokos*, 103–104.

17. *Acta Apostolicae Sedis* 10 (1919), 318.

6. Mary as Mediatrix of Grace

1. Odell, *Those Who Saw*, 51.

2. *Woman Clothed*, 55.

3. *Woman Clothed*, 55.

4. Odell, *Those Who Saw*, 72.

5. *Woman Clothed*, 60.

6. Odell, *Those Who Saw*, 76–77.

7. See Nicole Vray, *Un autre regard sur Marie: Histoire et religion* (Lyon: Olivetan, 2008), 86.

8. Fr. Joseph Dirwin, "Saint Catherine Labouré of the Miraculous Medal," EWTN, http://www.ewtn.com/library/mary/catlabou.htm.

9. Joseph I. Dirwin, C.M., "The Lady of the Miraculous Medal," in *Woman Clothed*, 77.

10. Dirwin, *Woman Clothed*, 83.

11. Dirwin, *Woman Clothed*, 83.

12. It should be noted that footnote 11 of Vatican II's 1962 *Schema Constitutionis Dogmaticae De Beata Maria Virgine Matre Dei et Matre Hominum* states that "the compassion of Mary has a connection with the redemption in such a way that she may rightly be called

co-redemptrix" (*compassio Mariae connexionem habet cum redemptione, talique modo ut ipsa inde merito dici possit corredemptrix*), *Acta Synodalia Sacrosancti Concilii Oecumenici Vaticani II, Volumen* I, *Periodus Prima, Pars* IV (Vatican City, 1971), 104. This schema also has an extensive footnote 16, which explains the history of the terms "Redemptrix" and "Co-Redemptrix" as applied to Mary. This footnote refers to the approval of the Marian title Co-Redemptrix by the Holy Office during the pontificate of St. Pius X and the use of this title by Pius XI on three separate occasions (*Acta Synodalia Sacrosancti Concilii Oecumenici Vaticani II, Volumen* I, *Periodus Prima, Pars* IV [Vatican City, 1971], 108). In the *praenotanda* to the 1962 schema, an explanation is given for why the term "Co-Redemptrix" is omitted in the actual text: "Certain terms and expressions used by Roman Pontiffs have been omitted, which, although most true in themselves (*in se verissima*), may be difficult for the separated brethren (such as the Protestants) to understand. Among such words the following may be enumerated: 'Coredemptrix of the human race' [St. Pius X, Pius XI]; 'Reparatrix of the whole world' [Leo XIII] ... etc." (*Acta Synodalia Sacrosancti Concilii Oecumenici Vaticani II, Volumen* I, *Periodus Prima, Pars* IV [Vatican City, 1971], 99).

13. Some reject the title Co-Redemptrix because they believe it implies a type of equivalence between Mary's contribution to redemption and that of Christ. However, this is not what the term means. The prefix "co" comes from the Latin *cum*, which means "with." Fr. Ludwig Ott, on pages 229–230 of his well-known text *The Fundamentals of Catholic Dogma* (London: Baronius Press, 2018), offers this comment: "The title *Coredemptrix* = Coredemptress, which has been current since the fifteenth century, and which also appears in some official Church documents under Pius X (cf. *AAS* 6 [1914] 108), must not be conceived in the sense of an equation of the efficacy of Mary with the redemptive activity of Christ, the sole Redeemer of humanity (1 Tim. 2, 5)."

14. *NWD-C*, 427.

15. Cf. Collation 6, 14, in his *Collations on the Seven Gifts of the Holy Spirit.*

16. Bonaventure, *De Nativit*, III (Third Sermon on the Nativity of the Blessed Virgin Mary), in St. Bonaventure, *Opera Omnia*, 10 vols. (Quaracchi: Collegium S. Bonaventurae, 1882–1902) Vol. 9, 713B.

17. S. Bonav. 1. Sent d. 48, *ad Litt. dub.* 4. (St. Bonaventure, Commentary on the First Book of the Sentences d. 48; on doubt 4) in *Opera Omnia* (Quaracchi ed.), Vol. 1, p. 801.

18. Eadmeri Mon, *De Excellentia Virg. Mariae,* c. 9, in J. P. Migne, ed. *Patrologiae Cursus Completus, Series Latina* (Paris: 1884ff.) 159: 573. (Hereafter, PL.)

19. Bernardine of Siena, *Quadragesimale de evangelio aeterno,* sermo X [given as *sermo* 51 in D-H 3370 footnote 4], in Bernardine of Siena, *Opera Omnia,* Vol. 4 (Quaracchi: Collegium S. Bonaventurae, 1956), 551.

20. Pius X, encyclical *Ad Diem Illum Laetissimum* (February 2, 1904), 13–14.

21. Gloria Falcão Dodd, *The Virgin Mary: Mediatrix of All Grace* (New Bedford, MA: Academy of the Immaculate, 2012), 101–110, 449.

22. The Dutch woman claimed that the apparitions continued from 1945 to 1959.

23. Ida Peerdeman, *The Messages of the Lady of All Nations* (Amsterdam: The Lady of All Nations Foundation, 1999), 99.

24. J. M. Punt, Statement of May 31, 2002, The Lady of All Nations, https://www.de-vrouwe.info/en/bishop2002. Accessed June 11, 2019.

25. Alessandro M. Apollonio, F.I., "Mary Mediatrix of All Graces," in Miravalle's *Mariology,* 444–451.

26. Cf. Mark Miravalle, "Mary Co-Redemptrix: A Dogmatic Crowning for the Queen?" August 22, 2011, https://dominicmedals.com/mary-co-redemtprix-a-dogmatic-crowning. Accessed June 3, 2019.

27. Benedict XVI, homily of May 11, 2007, in São Paulo, Brazil, n. 5,: http://w2.vatican.va/content/benedict-xvi/it/homilies/2007/documents/hf_ben-xvi_hom_20070511_canonization-brazil.html. Accessed June 11, 2019.

28. Benedict XVI, letter to Archbishop Zimowski (Jan. 10, 2013), http://w2.vatican.va/content/benedict-xvi/la/letters/2013/documents/hf_ben-xvi_let_20130110_card-zimowski.html.

7. Mary as Advocate

1. Abbé M. Richard, *What Happened at Pontmain* (Washington, NJ: Ave Maria Institute), 41, http://johnhaffert.org/wp-content/uploads/2013/08/What-Happened-at-Pontman.pdf.

2. Richard, *What Happened,* 24.

3. Richard, *What Happened*, 26.

4. Varghese, *God Sent*, 107.

5. Ingo Swann, *The Great Apparitions of Mary: An Examination of Twenty-Two Supranormal Appearances* (Agoura Hills, CA: Swann-Ryder Productions, 2018), 77.

6. Swann, *The Great Apparitions*, 78.

7. *Pilgrim Magazine*, No. 6976, August 11, 2016, 24.

8. Irenaeus, *Adversus haereses*, 5, 19, as cited in Gambero, *Mary and the Fathers*, 54.

9. Gambero, *Mary and the Fathers*, 56.

10. Gambero, *Mary and the Fathers*, 56.

11. Ephrem the Syrian, *De Laud. Dei Gen.*, as cited by Alphonsus Liguori in *The Glories of Mary*, ed. Eugene Grimm, C.Ss.R. (Brooklyn, NY: Redemptorist Fathers, 1931), 670.

12. Romanus the Singer, *Hymn on the Nativity* II, as cited in O'Carroll, *Theotokos*, 6.

13. O'Carroll, *Theotokos*, 6.

14. O'Carroll, *Theotokos*, 6.

15. The Latin reads, *Sub tuum praesidium confugimus, sancta Dei Genitrix. Nostras deprecationes ne despicias in necessitatibus nostris, sed a periculis cunctis libra nos semper, Virgo gloriosa et benedicta.* On September 29, 2018, Pope Francis asked all the faithful to recite this prayer along with the prayer to St. Michael the Archangel after every Rosary during the month of October to help protect the Church against the devil: https://www.vaticannews.va/en/pope/news/2018-09/pope-francis-pray-rosary-october.html.

16. Edward Sri, "Advocate and Queen," in Miravalle, *Mariology*, 488.

17. Augustine, *Sermon* 184; see O'Carroll, *Theotokos*, 6.

18. O'Carroll, *Theotokos*, 317. Although the *Salve Regina* has been attributed to St. Bernard of Clairvaux (1090–1153), it was more likely written by either Hermann the Lame, a monk of Reichenau (1013–1054), or Adhemar, bishop of Le Puy (d. 1098).

19. Buono, *Greatest Marian Prayers*, 49–50.

20. Translation taken from the Apostolic Penitentiary, *Manual of Indulgences: Norms and Grants*, 4th ed. (Washington, DC: United States Catholic Conference, 2016), 61.

21. J. P. Migne, ed. *Theotokos, Patrologiae Cursus Completus, Series Latina* (Paris: 1844ff.), vol. 183, 43C, cited in O'Carroll, *Theotokos* 6.

22. Sri, "Advocate and Queen," in Miravalle, *Mariology*, 489.

23. Pius VII, apostolic constitution *Tanto studio*, 42, in *Our Lady: Papal Teachings*, selected and arranged by the Benedictine Monks of Solesmes; trans. The Daughters of St. Paul (Boston: The Daughters of St. Paul, 1961), 165.

24. Pope Pius X, "Prayers of Pope Pius X to Mary," University of Dayton, https://udayton.edu/imri/mary/p/prayers-of-pope-pius-x-to-mary.php.

25. Pius XI, encyclical, *Miserentissimus Redemptor* (May 8, 1928), 21, in *Our Lady*, 209.

26. Pius XII, Radio Message to the National Marian Congress of Argentina (October 12, 1947), in *Our Lady*, 280. The citation from Suárez referring to Mary as "universal advocate" (*universalem advocatum*) is found in the Jesuit's treatise *De Mysteriis Vitae Christi disput. 23, sectio III, n. 5*, in Suárez's *Opera Omnia* (Paris: Ludovicus Vivès, 1856–1861), Vol. XIX, 336.

27. John Paul II, homily at the Shrine of Our Lady of the Rosary of Pompei (October 21, 1979), n. 4, http://w2.vatican.va/content/john-paul-ii/it/homilies/1979/documents/hf_jp-ii_hom_19791021_pompei.html. The Italian reads, *Maria è sempre al centro stesso della nostra preghiera. Essa è la prima fra coloro che chiedono. Ed è l' 'Omnipotentia supplex': l'Onnipotenza d'intercessione.* Translation taken from Rev. Arthur Burton Calkins, "Mary as Coredemptrix, Mediatrix and Advocate in the Contemporary Roman Liturgy," in *Mary: Coredemptrix, Mediatrix, Advocate: Theological Foundations towards a Papal Definition?* ed. Mark Miravalle (Santa Barbara, CA: Queenship Publishing, 1995), 96.

28. John Paul II, General Audience of September 24, 1997, 5, http://w2.vatican.va/content/john-paul-ii/en/audiences/1997/documents/hf_jp-ii_aud_24091997.html.

29. "Novena to Our Lady of Hope," EWTN, https://www.ewtn.com/devotionals/novena/hope.htm.

8. Mary as Mother of Mercy

1. John Paul II, "Letter of John Paul II to the Bishop of Liège on the 50th Anniversary of the Recognition of the Apparitions of Our Lady at Banneux" (July 31, 1999), 5, https://w2.vatican.va/content/john-paul-ii/en/letters/1999/documents/hf_jp-ii_let_19990731_banneux.html.

2. John Paul II, Letter to the Bishop of Liège (1999), 1.

3. Odell, *Those Who Saw*, 156.

4. Renee Laurentin and Patrick Sbalchiero, *Dizionario delle "apparizione" della Vergine Maria* (Edizioni Art, 2010), 105–106.

5. Laurentin and Sbalchiero, *Dizionario delle "apparizione,"* 106.

6. Louis-Joseph Kerkhofs, *Our Lady of Banneux: Studies and documents* (Leuven: Mont-César Abbey, 1950).

7. Robert Maloy, S.M., "The Virgin of the Poor," in *Woman Clothed*, 258.

8. See *NWD-C*, 433.

9. Maloy, "The Virgin of the Poor," in *Woman Clothed*, 264.

10. See the heading just before n. 12 of Benedict XVI's encyclical *Deus Caritas Est*, available at http://w2.vatican.va/content/benedict-xvi/en/encyclicals/documents/hf_ben-xvi_enc_20051225_deus-caritas-est.html.

11. Anthony Buono, *The Greatest Marian Titles: Their History, Meaning, and Usage* (Staten Island, NY: Alba House, 2008), 138. Some believe that "the abyss of mercy" comes from the Pseudo-Sophronius. See O'Carroll, *Theotokos*, 259.

12. O'Carroll, *Theotokos*, 259.

13. O'Carroll, *Theotokos*, 259.

14. Introduction to the Mass Formulary for "Holy Mary, Queen and Mother of Mercy," in *Collection of Masses of the Blessed Virgin Mary, Volume I: Missal*, prepared by the International Commission on English in the Liturgy and the Secretariat of Divine Worship, United States Conference of Catholic Bishops (Collegeville, MN: Liturgical Press, 2012), 242.

15. International Commission on English in the Liturgy and the Secretariat of Divine Worship, United States Conference of Catholic Bishops, *Collection of Masses*, 38.

16. Buono, *Greatest Marian Titles*, 143–144.

17. Lawrence of Brindisi, *Mariale*, Second Sermon on the *Salve Regina*, III: *Opera Omnia*, I (Padua: Seminary Press, 1928), 391.

18. Buono, *Greatest Marian Titles*, 144.

19. M. Faustina Kowalska, *Diary: Divine Mercy in My Soul* (Stockbridge, MA: Marians of the Immaculate Conception, 1999), 149, no. 330.

20. Adapted from Banneux Notre-Dame Sanctuaire de la Vierge des Pauvres (Belgique), https://www.banneux-nd.be/en/prayers-from-banneux. Accessed June 1, 2019.

9. Mary as Mother of the Church

1. Junno Arocho Esteves, "Pope to Canonize Fatima Seers May 13; October Date for Other Saints," Catholic News Service, April 20, 2017, https://www.catholicnews.com/services/englishnews/2017/pope-to-canonize-fatima-seers-may-13-october-date-for-other-saints.cfm.

2. Joseph Pronechen, "Sister Lucia of Fatima Takes Step toward Beatification," *National Catholic Register*, February 14, 2017, http://www.ncregister.com/blog/joseph-pronechen/sister-lucia-of-fatima-takes-step-toward-beatification.

3. Odell, *Those Who Saw*, 116.

4. Odell, *Those Who Saw*, 146.

5. Donald Calloway, M.I.C., "Five First Saturdays for Peace, Salvation," https://www.fathercalloway.com/13th-of-the-month-club/five-first-saturdays-for-peace.html.

6. "Pilgrim numbers" courtesy of Alliance of Religions and Conservation (ARC), June 2014, http://www.arcworld.org/projects.asp?projectID=500.

7. "Pontificate of Pope Francis Consecrated to Our Lady of Fatima," Catholic News Agency, May 14, 2013, https://www.catholicnewsagency.com/news/pontificate-of-pope-francis-consecrated-to-our-lady-of-fatima.

8. This refers to *Fatima in Lucia's Own Words* (Fatima, Portugal: Postulation Centre, 1976). See also Frère Antonio Maria Martins, *The Whole Truth about Fatima, Vol. I: Science and the Facts* (Buffalo, NY: Immaculate Heart Publications, 1989), 182.

9. "The Secret in Three Parts: The Second Part," Fatima Archive, http://archive.fatima.org/essentials/message/tspart2.asp.

10. Congregation for the Doctrine of the Faith, "The Message of Fatima" (June 26, 2000), http://www.vatican.va/roman_curia/congregations/cfaith/documents/rc_con_cfaith_doc_20000626_message-fatima_en.html.

11. Congregation for the Doctrine of the Faith, "The Message of Fatima."

12. Congregation for Divine Worship and the Discipline of the Sacraments, "Decree on the Celebration of the Blessed Virgin Mary Mother of the Church in the General Roman Calendar" (February 11, 2018), http://www.vatican.va/roman_curia/congregations/ccdds/documents/rc_con_ccdds_doc_20180211_decreto-mater-ecclesiae_en.html.

13. John Paul II, General Audience (Sept. 17, 1997), 3, http://w2.vatican.va/content/john-paul-ii/en/audiences/1997/documents/hf_jp-ii_aud_17091997.html.

14. The woman of Revelation 12 represents Israel and the Church, but the Marian dimension is also present because her son, "destined to rule all the nations with an iron rod," is revealed as "the King of kings and Lord of lords" in Revelation 19:15. Many popes have also identified Mary as the woman of Revelation 12. See John Paul II, *Redemptoris Mater*, 47.

15. Anselm of Canterbury, Oratio 52: PL 158, 956B–957A, as cited in Gambero, *Mary and the Fathers*, 116.

16. O'Carroll, *Theotokos*, 252.

17. O'Carroll, *Theotokos*, 252.

18. O'Carroll, *Theotokos*, 253.

19. O'Carroll, *Theotokos*, 252. See also Leo XIII, encyclical letter *Adiutricem* (September 5, 1895), n. 6, http://w2.vatican.va/content/leo-xiii/en/encyclicals/documents/hf_l-xiii_enc_05091895_adiutricem.html. Accessed June 3, 2019.

20. An earlier title of what would become Chapter VIII of *Lumen Gentium* was "On the Blessed Virgin Mary, Mother of the Church." It was changed, though, to its present title, "On the Blessed Virgin Mary, Mother of God, in the Mystery of Christ and the Church." About two hundred bishops asked that the earlier title be restored, but the Theological Commission responded by noting that the revised title better corresponded to the contents of the chapter.

21. *Lumen Gentium*, 53. This expression is taken from Benedict XIV's 1748 bull, *Gloriosae Dominae*.

22. Paul VI, allocution of November 21, 1964, 30, http://w2.vatican.va/content/paul-vi/it/speeches/1964/documents/hf_p-vi_spe_19641121_conclusions-iii-sessions.html.

23. Paul VI, allocution of November 21, 1964, 32.

24. International Commission on English in the Liturgy and the Secretariat of Divine Worship, United States Conference of Catholic Bishops, *Collection of Masses of the Blessed Virgin Mary, Mother of the Church in the General Roman Calendar*, 200–208.

25. Congregation for Divine Worship and the Discipline of the Sacraments, "Decree on the Celebration" (February 11, 2018).

26. Congregation for Divine Worship, and the Discipline of the Sacraments, "Decree on the Celebration" in the commentary following the decree.

27. Francis, "Prayer for Pilgrims to the Shrine of Our Lady of Fatima on the Occasion of the 100th Anniversary of the Apparitions," May 12–13, 2017, http://w2.vatican.va/content/francesco/en/prayers/documents/papa-francesco_preghiere_20170512_.

10. Mary as Queen of Heaven

1. From the Beauraing ruling documents, ed. Don Sharkey, *"I Will Convert Sinners: Our Lady's Apparitions at Beauraing, 1932–1933"* (Boston: Divine Word Publications, 1957), https://archive.org/stream/iwillconvertsinn00shar/iwillconvertsinn00shar_djvu.txt.

2. André-Marie Charue, "Bishop of Namur's Statement on Apparitions at Beauraing," The Miracle Hunter website, http://www.miraclehunter.com/marian_apparitions/statements/beauraing_statement.html.

3. *Sanctuaires de Beauraing,* https://www.sanctuairesdebeauraing.be/en/short-story. Accessed June 1, 2019.

4. *Sanctuaires de Beauraing.*

5. *Sanctuaires de Beauraing.*

6. *Sanctuaires de Beauraing.*

7. Sharkey, *"I Will Convert Sinners,"* 10.

8. Sharkey, *"I Will Convert Sinners,"* 16.

9. Sharkey, *"I Will Convert Sinners,"* 31.

10. Don Sharkey, "The Virgin with the Golden Heart," in *Woman Clothed,* 227.

11. Scott Hahn, *Hail, Holy Queen: The Mother of God in the Word of God* (New York: Doubleday, 2001), 81.

12. Sri, "Advocate and Queen," in Miravalle, *Mariology,* 484.

13. John Paul II, encyclical, *Redemptoris Mater* (March 25, 1987), n. 21, http://w2.vatican.va/content/john-paul-ii/en/encyclicals/documents/hf_jp-ii_enc_25031987_redemptoris-mater.html. Accessed June 3, 2019.

14. Sri, "Advocate and Queen," in Miravalle, *Mariology,* 482.

15. Sri, "Advocate and Queen," in Miravalle, *Mariology,* 492.

16. Pius XII, encyclical, *Ad Caeli Reginam* (Oct. 11, 1954), n. 10.

17. Pius XII, encyclical, *Ad Caeli Reginam* (Oct. 11, 1954), n. 17.

18. Pius XII, encyclical, *Ad Caeli Reginam* (Oct. 11, 1954), n. 20.

19. Sri, "Advocate and Queen," in Miravalle, *Mariology,* 493.

20. Sri, "Advocate and Queen," in Miravalle, *Mariology,* 495.

21. Sri, "Advocate and Queen," in Miravalle, *Mariology,* 495–496.

22. Pius XII, *Ad Caeli Reginam,* n. 23.

23. Pius XII, *Ad Caeli Reginam*, n. 23.

24. Sri, "Advocate and Queen," in Miravalle, *Mariology*, 496.

25. Pius XII, *Ad Caeli Reginam*, n. 24.

26. Sri, "Advocate and Queen," in Miravalle, *Mariology*, 497.

27. Pius XII, *Ad Caeli Reginam*, n. 34.

28. Pius XII, *Ad Caeli Reginam*, n. 34, n. 35.

29. Pius XII, *Ad Caeli Reginam*, n. 34, n. 37.

30. Adapted from a prayer in an article by Patti Armstrong, "The 'Golden Heart' Apparition of Our Lady of Beauraing" National Catholic Register website, August 10, 2016, http://www.ncregister.com/blog/armstrong/the-golden-heart-apparition-of-our-lady-of-beauraing. Accessed June 11, 2019.

Robert L. Fastiggi is professor of systemic theology at Sacred Heart Major Seminary in Detroit, Michigan, where he has served since 1999. He was professor of religious studies at St. Edward's University in Austin, Texas, from 1985 to 1999.

Fastiggi earned his master's degree in theology in 1976 and his PhD in theology in 1987, both from Fordham University. He has authored, coauthored, edited, or coedited more than a dozen books. He was executive editor of the 2009–2013 supplements to the *New Catholic Encyclopedia*. His work has appeared in *Our Sunday Visitor* and *The Priest*, and he has been interviewed on EWTN, Catholic Answers, and Ave Maria Radio.

Fastiggi is a member of the International Marian Association, a council member of the Mariological Society of America, and a corresponding member of the Pontifical Marian Academy International.

Fastiggi and his wife, Kathy, are parents of three adult children. They live in the Detroit area.

Michael O'Neill is the host of the weekly Relevant Radio Program *The Miracle Hunter*.

He is the author of *Exploring the Miraculous, 365 Days with Mary*, and *20 Questions: Apparitions and Revelations*. He has contributed to *Mater Misericordiae: An Annual Journal of Mariology*. He has appeared on NBC's *Today, The Dr. Oz Show, Fox and Friends, EWTN*, and numerous radio programs.

O'Neill was the consultant for the *National Geographic* December 2015 cover story about the Virgin Mary and was interviewed as the Marian expert on the corresponding television piece for *NatGeo Explorer*. O'Neill served as the expert commentator during the 2010 live broadcast of the approval of the Marian apparition at Champion, Wisconsin, as well as EWTN's coverage at the 100th Anniversary Mass of Our Lady of Fatima. He was the cohost of the television special *Miracle Hunters* on UpTV in 2015 and was a panelist for the twelve-part television series *Mary, Mother of All* on Shalom World. He is the creator and host of EWTN's *They Might Be Saints* about the lives of future saints and the search for canonization miracles.

O'Neill is a graduate of Stanford University and member of the Mariological Society of America and the Theological Commission of the International Marian Association.

Miraclehunter.com
Facebook: miraclehunteronline, themiraclehunter, 365DayswithMary, theymightbesaints
Twitter: @miraclehunter, @mightbesaints, @365dayswithmary
Instagram: miraclehuntercom
Pinterest: miraclehunter

AVE

AVE MARIA PRESS

Founded in 1865, Ave Maria Press,
a ministry of the Congregation of
Holy Cross, is a Catholic publishing
company that serves the spiritual and
formative needs of the Church and its
schools, institutions, and ministers;
Christian individuals and families; and
others seeking spiritual nourishment.

For a complete listing of titles from

Ave Maria Press

Sorin Books

Forest of Peace

Christian Classics

visit www.avemariapress.com

AVE MARIA PRESS
Notre Dame, IN
A Ministry of the United States Province of Holy Cross